Slow Cooker
Recipes

Publications International, Ltd.

Special thanks to the Campbell's Kitchen and Jane M. Freiman, Group Manager.

Pictured on the front cover: Slow Cooker Tuscan Beef Stew (*page 102*).

Pictured on the back cover (*left to right*): Slow Cooker Coq au Vin (*page 190*), Lentil Stew over Couscous (*page 97*), Apricot Glazed Pork Roast (*page 158*), and Wild Mushroom Beef Stew (*page 86*).

ISBN-13: 978-1-4508-2408-8

ISBN-10: 1-4508-2408-0

Library of Congress Control Number: 2011922389

Manufactured in China.

8 7 6 5 4 3 2 1

Preparation/Cooking Times: Preparation times are based on the approximate amount of time required to assemble the recipe before cooking, baking, chilling or serving. These times include preparation steps such as measuring, chopping and mixing. The fact that some preparations and cooking can be done simultaneously is taken into account. Preparation of optional ingredients and serving suggestions is not included.

table of contents

14

44

86

204

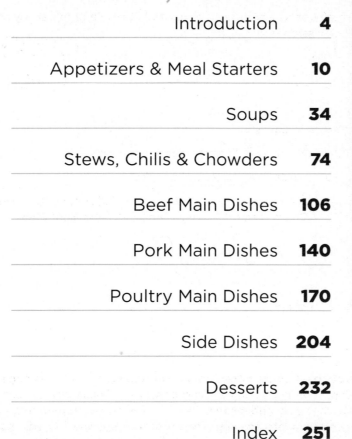

232

THE ORIGINAL SLOW COOKER

Campbell's soup
and the
CROCK-POT® slow cooker
—it's a match made in heaven.

Combining nearly 200 years of culinary experience from two leaders in convenient cooking solutions makes perfect sense. In fact, it's hard to believe this hasn't happened sooner.

Bringing together the CROCK-POT® slow cooker and the beloved products from Campbell offers you the best slow cooking has to offer. Within these pages you'll find great-tasting recipes using the trusted ingredients from *Campbell's*®, *Swanson*®, *Pace*®, *Prego*®, *Pepperidge Farm*®, and *V8*® all prepared in your CROCK-POT® slow cooker.

You'll also find tons of hints and tips that will make slow cooking a snap. Here's some basic information that will get you started.

Slow Cooker Sizes

Smaller slow cookers—such as 1- to 3½-quart models—are the perfect size for cooking for singles, a couple, or empty-nesters (and also for serving dips).

While medium-size slow cookers (those holding somewhere between 3 quarts and 5 quarts) will easily cook enough food at a time to feed a small family, they're also convenient for holiday side dishes or appetizers.

Large slow cookers are great for large family dinners, holiday entertaining, and potluck suppers. A 6-quart to 7-quart model is ideal if you like to make meals in advance, or have dinner tonight and store leftovers for another day.

Types of Slow Cookers

Current CROCK-POT® slow cookers come equipped with many different features and benefits, from auto cook programs to timed programming. Visit **www.crockpot.com** to find the slow cooker that best suits your needs.

How you plan to use a slow cooker may affect the model you choose to purchase—basic slow cookers can hold as little as 16 ounces or as much as 7 quarts. For everyday cooking, choose a size large enough to serve your family. If you plan to use the slow cooker primarily for entertaining, choose one of the larger sizes. The smallest sizes are great for keeping dips hot on a buffet, while the larger sizes can more readily fit large quantities of food and larger roasts.

Cooking, Stirring, and Food Safety

CROCK-POT® slow cookers are safe to leave unattended. The outer heating base may get hot as it cooks, but it should not pose a fire hazard. The heating element in the heating base functions at a low wattage and is safe for your countertops.

Most recipes call for your slow cooker to be filled about one-half to three-fourths full. Lean meats such as chicken or pork tenderloin will cook faster than meats with more connective tissue and fat, such as beef chuck or pork shoulder. Bone-in meats will take longer than boneless cuts. Typical slow cooker dishes take approximately 7 to 8 hours to reach the simmer point on LOW and about 3 to 4 hours on HIGH. Once the vegetables and meat start to simmer and braise, their flavors will fully blend and meat will become fall-off-the-bone tender.

According to the USDA, all bacteria are killed at a temperature of 165°F. To maintain that heat, it's important to follow the recommended cooking times and not to open the lid often, especially early in the cooking process when heat is building up inside the unit. If you need to open the lid to check on your food or are adding additional ingredients, remember to allow additional cooking time if necessary to ensure food is cooked through and tender.

Large slow cookers, the 6- to 7-quart sizes, may benefit with a quick stir halfway during cook time to help distribute heat and promote even cooking. However, it's usually unnecessary to stir at all—even ½ cup of liquid will help to distribute heat, and the crockery is the perfect medium for holding food at an even temperature throughout the cooking process.

Oven-Safe

All CROCK-POT® slow cooker removable crockery inserts may (without their lids) be used safely in ovens at up to 400°F. Also, all CROCK-POT® slow cookers are microwavable without their lids. If you own another brand slow cooker, please refer to your owner's manual for specific crockery cooking medium tolerances.

Frozen Food

Frozen food or partially frozen food can be successfully cooked in a slow cooker; however, it will require longer cooking than the same recipe made with fresh food. It's almost always preferable to thaw frozen food prior to placing it in the slow cooker. Using an instant-read thermometer is recommended to ensure meat is fully cooked through.

Pasta and Rice

If you're converting a recipe that calls for uncooked pasta, cook the pasta on the stovetop just until slightly tender before adding to the slow cooker. If you are converting a recipe that calls for cooked rice, stir in raw rice with other ingredients; add ¼ cup extra liquid per ¼ cup of raw rice.

Beans

Beans must be softened completely before combining with sugar and/or acidic foods. Sugar and acid have a hardening effect on beans and will prevent softening. Fully cooked canned beans may be used as a substitute for dried beans.

Vegetables

Root vegetables often cook more slowly than meat. Cut vegetables accordingly to cook at the same rate as meat—large or small, or lean versus marbled—and place near the sides or bottom of the stoneware to facilitate cooking.

Herbs

Fresh herbs add flavor and color when added at the end of the cooking cycle; if added at the beginning, many fresh herbs' flavor will dissipate over long cook times. Ground and/or dried herbs and spices work well in slow cooking and may be added at the beginning, and for dishes with shorter cook times, hearty fresh herbs such as rosemary and thyme hold up well. The flavor power of all herbs and spices can vary greatly depending on their particular strength and shelf life. Use chili powders and garlic powder sparingly, as these can sometimes intensify over the long cook times. Always taste the dish at end of the cook cycle and correct seasonings including salt and pepper.

Liquids

It is not necessary to use more than ½ to 1 cup liquid in most instances since juices in meats and vegetables are retained more in slow cooking than in conventional cooking. Excess liquid can be cooked down and concentrated after slow cooking on the stovetop or by removing meat and vegetables from stoneware, stirring in one of the following thickeners, and setting the slow cooker to HIGH. Cook on HIGH for approximately 15 minutes until juices are thickened.

Flour: All-purpose flour is often used to thicken soups or stews. Place flour in a small bowl or cup and stir in enough cold water to make a thin, lump-free mixture. With the slow cooker on HIGH, quickly stir the flour mixture into the liquid in the slow cooker. Cook, stirring frequently, until the mixture thickens.

Cornstarch: Cornstarch gives sauces a clear, shiny appearance; it is used most often for sweet dessert sauces and stir-fry sauces. Place cornstarch in a small bowl or cup and stir in cold water, stirring until the cornstarch dissolves. Quickly stir this mixture into the liquid in the slow cooker; the sauce will thicken as soon as the liquid boils. Cornstarch breaks down with too much heat, so never add it at the beginning of the slow cooking process, and turn off the heat as soon as the sauce thickens.

Arrowroot: Arrowroot (or arrowroot flour) comes from the root of a tropical plant that is dried and ground to a powder; it produces a thick clear sauce. Those who are allergic to wheat often use it in place of flour. Place arrowroot in a small bowl or cup and stir in cold water until the mixture is smooth. Quickly stir this mixture into the liquid in the slow cooker. Arrowroot thickens below the

boiling point, so it even works well in a slow cooker on LOW. Too much stirring can break down an arrowroot mixture.

Tapioca: Tapioca is a starchy substance extracted from the root of the cassava plant. Its greatest advantage is that it withstands long cooking, making it an ideal choice for slow cooking. Add it at the beginning of cooking and you'll get a clear thickened sauce in the finished dish. Dishes using tapioca as a thickener are best cooked on the LOW setting; tapioca may become stringy when boiled for a long time.

Milk

Milk, cream, and sour cream break down during extended cooking. When possible, add during last 15 to 30 minutes of cooking, until just heated through. Condensed soups may be substituted for milk and can cook for extended times.

Fish

Fish is delicate and should be stirred in gently during the last 15 to 30 minutes of cooking time. Cook until just cooked through and serve immediately.

Baked Goods

If you wish to prepare bread, cakes, or pudding cakes in a slow cooker, you may want to purchase a covered, vented metal cake pan accessory for your slow cooker. You can also use any straight-sided soufflé dish or deep cake pan that will fit into the ceramic insert of your unit. Baked goods can be prepared directly in the insert; however, they can be a little difficult to remove from the insert, so follow the recipe directions carefully.

Savor these great recipes from these two great brands, and let your family come home to a warm, welcoming dinner tonight.

appetizers & meal starters

Caponata

MAKES ABOUT 5¼ CUPS

PREP TIME
20 TO 25 MINUTES

COOK TIME
7 TO 8 HOURS (LOW)

1 medium eggplant (about 1 pound), peeled and cut into ½-inch pieces

1 can (about 14 ounces) diced Italian plum tomatoes, undrained

1 medium onion, chopped

1 red bell pepper, cut into ½-inch pieces

½ cup **Pace**® Salsa

¼ cup extra-virgin olive oil

2 tablespoons capers, drained

2 tablespoons balsamic vinegar

3 cloves garlic, minced

1 teaspoon dried oregano

¼ teaspoon salt

⅓ cup packed fresh basil, cut into thin strips

Toasted sliced Italian **or** French bread

1. Mix eggplant, tomatoes with juice, onion, bell pepper, salsa, oil, capers, vinegar, garlic, oregano and salt in **CROCK-POT**® slow cooker.

2. Cover; cook on LOW 7 to 8 hours or until vegetables are crisp-tender.

3. Stir in basil. Serve at room temperature with toasted bread.

Recipe courtesy of
Crock-Pot® Slow Cooker Kitchens

Asian Chicken Fondue

MAKES 6 TO 8 SERVINGS

PREP TIME
30 MINUTES

COOK TIME
4½ TO 5 HOURS (LOW)

1 cup shiitake mushrooms, stems removed

2 cups **Swanson**® Chicken Broth (Regular, **Natural Goodness**® *or* Certified Organic)

1 tablespoon teriyaki sauce

1 small leek (white *and* green parts), cleaned, trimmed and chopped

1 head baby bok choy, trimmed and roughly chopped

1 tablespoon mirin

2 tablespoons oyster sauce

1 tablespoon canola oil

2 pounds boneless, skinless chicken breasts, cut into 1-inch cubes
Salt *and* black pepper

1 cup peeled, seeded and cubed butternut squash

1 tablespoon cornstarch

2 tablespoons cold water

1 can (8 ounces) baby corn, drained

1 can (8 ounces) water chestnuts, drained

1. Combine mushrooms, chicken broth, teriyaki sauce, leek, bok choy, mirin and oyster sauce in **CROCK-POT**® slow cooker. Cover and cook on LOW while following remaining instructions.

2. Heat oil in large skillet over medium-high heat. Season chicken with salt and pepper. Add to pan; cook without stirring until browned on bottom, about 4 minutes. Turn and brown other side. Stir into sauce in **CROCK-POT**® slow cooker. Stir in butternut squash.

3. Cover and continue cooking on LOW 4½ to 5 hours. Twenty minutes before end of cooking, stir cornstarch into cold water; set aside. Stir baby corn and water chestnuts into **CROCK-POT**® slow cooker, then stir in cornstarch mixture. Cover and continue cooking on LOW. Serve with bamboo skewers, fondue forks or tongs so guests may serve themselves as desired. Broth may also be served in small soup bowls.

Recipe courtesy of
Crock-Pot® Slow Cooker Kitchens

Chicken Croustade

MAKES 6 TO 8 SERVINGS

PREP TIME
45 MINUTES

COOK TIME
3½ HOURS (LOW)

2 tablespoons canola oil

1½ pounds boneless, skinless chicken breasts, cut into ¼-inch pieces

Salt **and** black pepper

1 large portobello mushroom cap

1 shallot, minced

¼ cup white wine

1 tablespoon chopped fresh thyme

¼ teaspoon sweet paprika

¼ teaspoon ground cumin

¼ cup **Swanson**® Chicken Broth (Regular, **Natural Goodness**® **or** Certified Organic)

1 package (10 ounces) **Pepperidge Farm**® Puff Pastry Shells

1 egg yolk

2 tablespoons cream

3 tablespoons freshly grated Parmesan cheese

Minced and whole chives (optional)

1. Heat oil in large skillet over medium-high heat. Season chicken with salt and pepper and add to skillet with oil. Allow chicken to brown, untouched, about 4 minutes. Turn gently and brown other side.

2. Meanwhile, scrape gills from mushroom cap with spoon and discard. Chop mushroom cap into ¼-inch pieces.

3. Transfer chicken to **CROCK-POT**® slow cooker. Return skillet to heat and add shallot. Cook until shallot softens, 1 to 2 minutes. Stir in wine, scraping up any brown bits with wooden spoon. Continue to cook until wine is reduced to **about 2 tablespoons**, then pour over chicken. Stir in chopped mushroom, thyme, paprika, cumin and broth. Add pinch of salt and black pepper. Cover and cook on LOW 3 hours.

4. Two hours after starting to cook chicken, cook puff pastry shells according to package directions and cool completely.

Recipe courtesy of
***Crock-Pot® Slow Cooker
Kitchens***

5. Twenty minutes before end of cooking time, beat egg yolk and cream together. Stir **1 tablespoon** hot cooking liquid into egg mixture. Beat until well combined, then stir into remaining cooking liquid. Continue cooking on LOW, uncovered, 20 minutes. Stir in Parmesan cheese and turn off **CROCK·POT®** slow cooker. Divide chicken filling among puff pastry shells. Serve garnished with chives.

Mini Carnitas Tacos

**MAKES
12 SERVINGS
(36 MINI TACOS)**

PREP TIME
20 MINUTES

COOK TIME
6 HOURS (LOW)
OR 3 HOURS (HIGH)

1½ pounds boneless pork loin, cut into 1-inch cubes

1 onion, finely chopped

½ cup **Swanson®** Chicken Broth (Regular, **Natural Goodness®** *or* Certified Organic)

1 tablespoon chili powder

2 teaspoons ground cumin

1 teaspoon dried oregano

½ teaspoon minced chipotle pepper in adobo sauce

½ cup **Pace®** Pico de Gallo

2 tablespoons chopped fresh cilantro

½ teaspoon salt

12 (6-inch) flour *or* corn tortillas

¾ cup shredded sharp Cheddar cheese (optional)

3 tablespoons sour cream (optional)

1. Combine pork, onion, broth, chili powder, cumin, oregano and chipotle in **CROCK-POT®** slow cooker. Cover and cook on LOW 6 hours or on HIGH 3 hours or until pork is very tender. Pour off excess cooking liquid.

2. Shred pork with 2 forks; stir in pico de gallo, cilantro and salt. Cover and keep warm on LOW or WARM until serving.

3. Cut **3** circles from each tortilla with 2-inch biscuit cutter. Top **each** with some pork and garnish as desired with Cheddar cheese and sour cream. Serve warm.

tip

Carnitas, or "little meats" in Spanish, are a festive way to spice up any gathering. Carnitas traditionally include a large amount of lard, but slow cooking makes the dish more healthful by eliminating the need to add lard, oil or fat, while keeping the meat tender and tasteful.

Recipe courtesy of
Crock-Pot® Slow Cooker Kitchens

CROCK·POT®
· THE ORIGINAL SLOW COOKER ·

Campbell's

Sausage and Swiss Chard Stuffed Mushrooms

MAKES 6 TO 8 SERVINGS

PREP TIME
20 MINUTES

COOK TIME
3 HOURS (HIGH)

2 packages (6 ounces *each*) baby portobello mushrooms *or* large brown stuffing mushrooms*

4 tablespoons extra-virgin olive oil, divided

½ teaspoon salt, divided

½ teaspoon black pepper, divided

½ pound bulk pork sausage

½ onion, finely chopped

2 cups chopped Swiss chard, rinsed

¼ teaspoon dried thyme

2 tablespoons garlic-and-herb-flavored dried bread crumbs

1½ cups **Swanson**® Chicken Broth (Regular, **Natural Goodness**® *or* Certified Organic), divided

2 tablespoons grated Parmesan cheese

2 tablespoons chopped fresh parsley

Use "baby bellas" or cremini mushrooms. Do not substitute white button mushrooms.

1. Coat **CROCK-POT**® slow cooker with nonstick cooking spray. Wipe mushrooms clean, remove stems and hollow out mushroom caps. Pour **3 tablespoons** oil into small bowl. Brush mushrooms inside and out with oil. Season mushrooms with ¼ **teaspoon** salt and ¼ **teaspoon** pepper; set aside.

2. Heat remaining **1 tablespoon** oil in medium skillet over medium heat until hot. Add sausage. Cook and stir until browned. Transfer sausage with slotted spoon to medium bowl.

3. Add onion to skillet. Cook and stir, loosening browned bits, about 3 minutes or until translucent. Stir in chard and thyme. Cook until chard is just wilted, about 1 to 2 minutes.

4. Remove skillet from heat. Add sausage, bread crumbs, **1 tablespoon** broth, remaining ¼ **teaspoon** salt and remaining ¼ **teaspoon** pepper. Mix well to combine. Scoop **1 tablespoon** stuffing into each mushroom cap. Divide remaining stuffing evenly among mushrooms.

tip

If desired, place a small square of sliced Swiss cheese on each mushroom and continue cooking 15 minutes longer or until cheese is melted. Proceed as directed.

Recipe courtesy of Crock-Pot® Slow Cooker Kitchens

5. Pour remaining broth into **CROCK-POT®** slow cooker. Arrange
stuffed mushrooms in bottom. Cover; cook on HIGH 3 hours or until
mushrooms are tender. To serve, remove mushrooms with slotted
spoon; discard cooking liquid. Blend cheese and parsley and sprinkle
onto mushrooms.

Mini Swiss Steak Sandwiches

MAKES 16 TO 18 SERVINGS

PREP TIME
15 MINUTES

COOK TIME
3½ HOURS (HIGH)

2   tablespoons all-purpose flour

¼   teaspoon salt

¼   teaspoon black pepper

1¾ pounds boneless beef chuck steak, about 1 inch thick

2   tablespoons vegetable oil

1   medium onion, sliced

1   green bell pepper, sliced

1   clove garlic, sliced

1   cup stewed tomatoes

¾   cup **Campbell's®** Condensed Beef Broth, undiluted

2   teaspoons Worcestershire sauce

1   bay leaf

2   tablespoons cornstarch

2   packages (12 ounces **each**) sweet Hawaiian-style dinner rolls

1. Coat **CROCK-POT®** slow cooker with nonstick cooking spray. Combine flour, salt and pepper in large resealable food storage bag. Add steak; shake to coat.

2. Heat oil in large skillet over high heat. Add steak and brown on both sides. Transfer to **CROCK-POT®** slow cooker.

3. Add onion and bell pepper to skillet; cook and stir over medium-high heat 3 minutes or until softened. Add garlic; cook and stir 30 seconds. Pour mixture over steak.

4. Add tomatoes, broth, Worcestershire sauce and bay leaf. Cover; cook on HIGH 3½ hours or until steak is tender. Transfer steak to cutting board. Remove and discard bay leaf.

5. Blend cornstarch with **2 tablespoons** cooking liquid in small bowl until smooth. Stir into cooking liquid in **CROCK-POT®** slow cooker and continue cooking 10 minutes or until thickened.

6. Thinly slice steak against the grain to shred. Return steak to **CROCK-POT®** slow cooker. Serve steak mixture on rolls.

tip

Browning meat and poultry before cooking them in the CROCK-POT® slow cooker isn't necessary but helps to enhance the flavor and appearance of the finished dish.

Recipe courtesy of
Crock-Pot® Slow Cooker Kitchens

Artichoke and Nacho Cheese Dip

MAKES ABOUT 1 QUART

PREP TIME
5 MINUTES

COOK TIME
2 HOURS (LOW)

2 cans (10¾ ounces *each*) **Campbell's®** Condensed Fiesta Nacho Cheese Soup, undiluted

1 can (14 ounces) quartered artichoke hearts, drained and coarsely chopped

1 cup (4 ounces) shredded *or* thinly sliced pepper jack cheese

1 can (4 ounces) evaporated milk

2 tablespoons minced chives, divided

½ teaspoon paprika

Pepperidge Farm® Assorted Crackers *or* chips

1. Combine soup, artichoke hearts, cheese, milk, **1 tablespoon** chives and paprika in **CROCK-POT®** slow cooker. Cover; cook on LOW 2 hours.

2. Stir well. Sprinkle with remaining **1 tablespoon** chives and serve with crackers.

Recipe courtesy of
Crock-Pot® Slow Cooker Kitchens

THE ORIGINAL SLOW COOKER

Easy Party Meatballs

- **3** cups (1 pound 10 ounces) **Prego®** Marinara Italian Sauce
- **1** jar (12 ounces) grape jelly
- **½** cup prepared chili sauce
- **2½** pounds frozen fully-cooked meatballs, cocktail size

1. Stir the Italian sauce, jelly, chili sauce and meatballs in a 4½-quart **CROCK-POT®** slow cooker.

2. Cover and cook on LOW for 6 to 7 hours* or until the meatballs are cooked through. Serve the meatballs on a serving plate with toothpicks.

Or on HIGH for 3 to 4 hours.

MAKES 8 SERVINGS
PREP TIME 5 MINUTES
COOK TIME 6 HOURS

tips

*Larger-size **or** turkey meatballs can also be used, if desired.*

For a special touch, serve with cranberry chutney for dipping.

Recipe courtesy of
Campbell's Kitchen

Pork Meatballs in Garlicky Almond Sauce

**MAKES 6 SERVINGS
(4 MEATBALLS EACH)**

COOK TIME
3 TO 4 HOURS (HIGH)

½ cup blanched whole almonds

1 cup **Swanson**® Chicken Broth (Regular, **Natural Goodness**® *or* Certified Organic)

⅓ cup roasted red pepper

4 teaspoons minced garlic, divided

1 teaspoon salt, divided

½ teaspoon saffron threads (optional)

1 cup fresh bread crumbs, divided

¼ cup dry white wine *or* **Swanson**® Chicken Broth (Regular, **Natural Goodness**® *or* Certified Organic)

1 pound ground pork

¼ cup finely chopped onion

1 egg, lightly beaten

3 tablespoons minced fresh parsley

1. Place almonds in food processor; process until finely ground. Add broth, red pepper, **2 teaspoons** garlic, ½ **teaspoon** salt and saffron, if desired; process until smooth. Stir in ¼ **cup** bread crumbs. Transfer to **CROCK-POT**® slow cooker.

2. Place ¾ **cup** bread crumbs in large bowl; sprinkle with wine and stir gently. Add pork, onion, egg, parsley, remaining **2 teaspoons** garlic and ½ **teaspoon** salt; mix well. Form pork mixture into **24** (1-inch) balls.

3. Coat a large skillet with nonstick cooking spray and place over medium-high heat. Working in batches, cook meatballs turning to brown on all sides. Transfer to **CROCK-POT**® slow cooker with sauce as batches are done. Cover; cook on HIGH 3 to 4 hours or until meatballs are cooked through.

Recipe courtesy of
Crock-Pot® Slow Cooker Kitchens

Thai Coconut Chicken Meatballs

MAKES 4 TO 5 SERVINGS

PREP TIME
30 MINUTES

COOK TIME
3¾ HOURS TO
4¼ HOURS (HIGH)

1 pound ground chicken

2 green onions (white **and** green parts), chopped

1 clove garlic, minced

2 teaspoons toasted sesame oil

1 teaspoon fish sauce

2 teaspoons mirin

1 tablespoon canola oil

½ cup unsweetened canned coconut milk

¼ cup **Swanson**® Chicken Broth (Regular, **Natural Goodness**® *or* Certified Organic)

1 teaspoon Thai red curry paste

2 teaspoons packed brown sugar

2 teaspoons lime juice

1 tablespoon cornstarch

2 tablespoons cold water

tip

*Meatballs that are of equal size will cook at the same rate and be done at the same time. To ensure your meatballs are the same size, pat seasoned ground meat into an even rectangle and then slice into even rows and columns. Roll **each** portion into smooth ball.*

1. Combine chicken, green onions, garlic, sesame oil, fish sauce and mirin in large bowl. Mix well to combine and shape into meatballs about 1½ inches in diameter.

2. Heat canola oil in large skillet over medium-high heat. Add meatballs and cook, rolling to brown on all sides. Transfer to **CROCK-POT**® slow cooker. Add coconut milk, chicken broth, curry paste and sugar. Cover; cook on HIGH 3½ to 4 hours. Stir in lime juice.

3. Stir cornstarch into cold water, mixing until smooth. Stir in additional water as needed to reach consistency of heavy cream. Stir into sauce in **CROCK-POT**® slow cooker. Cook uncovered 10 to 15 minutes until sauce is slightly thickened and evenly coats meatballs.

Recipe courtesy of
Crock-Pot® Slow Cooker Kitchens

Mahogany Wings

MAKES 18 WINGS

PREP TIME
6 HOURS 30 MINUTES

COOK TIME
4 HOURS

6   pounds chicken wings (about 36 wings)

1   can (10½ ounces) **Campbell's**® Condensed Beef Broth

2   bunches green onions, chopped

1   cup soy sauce

1   cup plum sauce

6   cloves garlic, minced

½   cup light molasses **or** honey

¼   cup cider vinegar

1   tablespoon cornstarch

1. Cut off the chicken wing ends and discard. Cut the chicken wings in half at the joint.

2. Stir the broth, onions, soy sauce, plum sauce, garlic, molasses and vinegar in a large nonmetallic bowl. Add the chicken and stir to coat. Cover and refrigerate for 6 hours or overnight.

3. Stir ½ **cup** of the marinade and the cornstarch in a small bowl. Add the cornstarch and chicken mixture to a 6-quart **CROCK-POT**® slow cooker.

4. Cover and cook on HIGH for 4 to 5 hours* or until the chicken is cooked through.

Or on LOW for 7 to 8 hours.

Recipe courtesy of
Campbell's Kitchen

Refried Bean Dip with Blue Tortilla Chips

3 cans (16 ounces **each**) refried beans

1 cup **Pace**® Picante Sauce

½ teaspoon salt

½ teaspoon black pepper

3 cups shredded Cheddar cheese, divided

¾ cup chopped green onions

2 packages (12 ounces **each**) blue tortilla chips

MAKES 10 SERVINGS

COOK TIME
2 TO 4 HOURS (LOW)

Combine refried beans, picante sauce, salt and pepper in large bowl. Spread ⅓ of bean mixture on bottom of **CROCK-POT**® slow cooker. Sprinkle evenly with **¾ cup** cheese. Repeat layers, finishing with cheese layer. Sprinkle green onions evenly on cheese. Cover; cook on LOW 2 to 4 hours. Serve with blue tortilla chips for dipping.

Recipe courtesy of
Crock-Pot® **Slow Cooker Kitchens**

appetizers & meal starters

29

Swiss Cheese Fondue

MAKES 6 SERVINGS

PREP TIME
10 MINUTES

COOK TIME
1 HOUR

1 clove garlic, cut in half

1 can (10½ ounces) **Campbell's**® Condensed Chicken Broth

2 cans (10¾ ounces *each*) **Campbell's**® Condensed Cheddar Cheese Soup

1 cup water

½ cup Chablis *or* other dry white wine

1 tablespoon Dijon-style mustard

1 tablespoon cornstarch

4 cups shredded Emmentaler *or* Gruyère cheese (about 1 pound), at room temperature

¼ teaspoon ground nutmeg

Dash ground black pepper

Pepperidge Farm® Garlic Bread, prepared and cut into cubes

Fresh vegetables

tip

This recipe may be doubled.

1. Rub the inside of a 5½-quart **CROCK-POT**® slow cooker with the cut sides of the garlic. Discard the garlic. Stir the broth, soup, water, wine, mustard, cornstarch, cheese, nutmeg and black pepper in the cooker.

2. Cover and cook on LOW for 1 hour or until the cheese is melted, stirring occasionally.

3. Serve with the bread and vegetables on skewers for dipping.

Recipe courtesy of
Campbell's Kitchen

Chicken & Vegetable Bruschetta

MAKES 7 CUPS

PREP TIME
15 MINUTES

COOK TIME
6 HOURS

STAND TIME
5 MINUTES

1 can (10¾ ounces) **Campbell's®** Condensed Cream of Mushroom Soup (Regular **or** 98% Fat Free)

1 can (about 14.5 ounces) diced tomatoes, drained

1 small eggplant, peeled and diced (about 2 cups)

1 large zucchini, diced (about 2 cups)

1 small onion, chopped (about ¼ cup)

1 pound skinless, boneless chicken breast halves

¼ cup shredded Parmesan cheese

2 tablespoons chopped fresh parsley **or** basil leaves

Thinly sliced Italian bread, toasted

1. Stir the soup, tomatoes, eggplant, zucchini and onion in a 6-quart **CROCK-POT®** slow cooker. Add the chicken and turn to coat.

2. Cover and cook on LOW for 6 to 7 hours* or until the chicken is fork-tender.

3. Remove the chicken from the **CROCK-POT®** slow cooker to a cutting board and let stand for 5 minutes. Using 2 forks, shred the chicken. Return the chicken to the **CROCK-POT®** slow cooker. Stir in the cheese and parsley.

4. Serve on the bread slices. Sprinkle with additional Parmesan cheese and chopped parsley, if desired.

Or on HIGH for 4 to 5 hours.

tip

*The chicken mixture is also delicious over hot cooked rice **or** pasta.*

Recipe courtesy of
Campbell's Kitchen

Hot Broccoli Cheese Dip

½ cup (1 stick) butter

6 stalks celery, sliced

2 onions, chopped

2 cans (4 ounces **each**) sliced mushrooms, drained

¼ cup **plus** 2 tablespoons all-purpose flour

2 cans (10¾ ounces **each**) **Campbell's®** Condensed Cream of Celery Soup (Regular **or** 98% Fat Free)

5 to 6 ounces garlic cheese, cut into cubes

2 packages (10 ounces **each**) frozen broccoli spears

French bread slices, bell pepper strips, cherry tomatoes

1. Melt butter in large skillet. Add celery, onions and mushrooms; cook and stir until translucent. Stir in flour and cook 2 to 3 minutes. Transfer to **CROCK-POT®** slow cooker.

2. Stir in soup, cheese and broccoli. Cover; cook on HIGH, stirring every 15 minutes, until cheese is melted. Turn **CROCK-POT®** slow cooker to LOW. Cover; cook 2 to 4 hours or until ready to serve.

3. Serve warm with bread slices and assorted vegetables.

MAKES ABOUT 6 CUPS
PREP TIME
10 TO 15 MINUTES
COOK TIME
30 MINUTES TO 1 HOUR (HIGH) PLUS 2 TO 4 HOURS (LOW)

Recipe courtesy of
Crock-Pot® Slow Cooker Kitchens

soups

Winter Squash Soup

MAKES 8 SERVINGS

PREP TIME
20 MINUTES

COOK TIME
7 HOURS 10 MINUTES

5¼ cups **Swanson**® Chicken Broth (Regular, **Natural Goodness**® *or* Certified Organic)

¼ cup packed brown sugar

2 tablespoons minced fresh ginger root

1 cinnamon stick

1 butternut squash (about 1¾ pounds), peeled, seeded and cut into 1-inch pieces (about 4 cups)

1 large acorn squash, peeled, seeded and cut into 1-inch pieces (about 3½ cups)

1 large sweet onion, coarsely chopped (about 1 cup)

1. Stir the broth, brown sugar, ginger root, cinnamon stick, squash and onion in a 6-quart **CROCK-POT**® slow cooker.

2. Cover and cook on LOW for 7 to 8 hours or until the squash is tender.

3. Remove the cinnamon stick. Place ⅓ of the squash mixture into a blender or food processor. Cover and blend until smooth. Pour the mixture into a 4-quart saucepan. Repeat the blending process twice more with the remaining squash mixture. Cook over medium heat until the mixture is hot.

Creamy Winter Squash Soup: Stir in ½ **cup** of half-and-half before reheating the soup in step 3.

Recipe courtesy of
Campbell's Kitchen

Chicken & Herb Dumplings

soups

36

MAKES 8 SERVINGS

PREP TIME
20 MINUTES

COOK TIME
7 HOURS 45 MINUTES

2 pounds skinless, boneless chicken breasts **and/or** thighs, cut into 1-inch pieces

5 medium carrots, cut into 1-inch pieces (about 2½ cups)

4 stalks celery, cut into 1-inch pieces (about 2 cups)

2 cups frozen whole kernel corn

3½ cups **Swanson®** Chicken Stock

¼ teaspoon ground black pepper

¼ cup all-purpose flour

½ cup water

2 cups all-purpose baking mix

⅔ cup milk

1 tablespoon chopped fresh rosemary leaves **or** 1 teaspoon dried rosemary leaves, crushed

tip

Leaving the lid slightly ajar prevents condensation from dripping onto the dumplings during cooking.

1. Stir the chicken, carrots, celery, corn, stock and black pepper in a 6-quart **CROCK-POT®** slow cooker.

2. Cover and cook on LOW for 7 to 8 hours* or until the chicken is cooked through.

3. Stir the flour and water in a small bowl until the mixture is smooth. Stir the flour mixture in the **CROCK-POT®** slow cooker. Turn the heat to HIGH. Cover and cook for 5 minutes or until the mixture boils and thickens.

4. Stir the baking mix, milk and rosemary in a medium bowl. Drop the batter by rounded tablespoonfuls over the chicken mixture. Tilt the lid to vent and cook on HIGH for 40 minutes or until the dumplings are cooked in the center.

*Or on HIGH for 4 to 5 hours.

Recipe courtesy of
Campbell's Kitchen

Lentil and Portobello Soup

2 portobello mushrooms (about 8 ounces *total*), cleaned and trimmed

1 tablespoon olive oil

1 medium onion, chopped

2 medium carrots, cut into ½-inch-thick rounds

2 cloves garlic, minced

1 cup dried lentils

1 can (28 ounces) diced tomatoes in juice, undrained

1 can (14½ ounces) **Swanson**® Vegetable Broth (Regular *or* Certified Organic)

1 teaspoon dried rosemary

1 bay leaf

Salt

Black pepper

1. Remove stems from mushrooms; coarsely chop stems. Cut each cap in half, then cut each half into ½-inch pieces. Set aside.

2. Heat oil in large skillet over medium heat. Add onion, carrots and garlic and cook, stirring occasionally, until onion softens. Transfer to **CROCK-POT**® slow cooker. Layer lentils, tomatoes with juice, vegetable broth, mushroom caps and stems, dried rosemary and bay leaf on top of carrots and onion. Cover; cook on HIGH 5 to 6 hours or until lentils are tender. Remove bay leaf and season to taste with salt and pepper before serving. Serve hot.

Recipe courtesy of
Crock-Pot® Slow Cooker Kitchens

soups

38

Pasta Fagioli Soup

MAKES 5 TO 6 SERVINGS

PREP TIME
12 MINUTES

COOK TIME
4 TO 5 HOURS (LOW)

2 cans (about 14 ounces *each*) **Swanson**® 50% Less Sodium Beef Broth *or* **Swanson**® Vegetable Broth (Regular *or* Certified Organic)

1 can (about 15 ounces) Great Northern beans, rinsed and drained

1 can (about 14 ounces) diced tomatoes

2 zucchini, quartered lengthwise and sliced

1 tablespoon olive oil

1½ teaspoons minced garlic

½ teaspoon dried basil

½ teaspoon dried oregano

½ cup *uncooked* tubetti, ditalini *or* small shell pasta

½ cup garlic seasoned croutons

½ cup grated Asiago *or* Romano cheese

3 tablespoons chopped fresh basil *or* Italian parsley (optional)

tip

Only small pasta varieties like tubetti, ditalini or small shell-shaped pasta should be used in this recipe. The low heat of a CROCK-POT® slow cooker won't allow larger pasta shapes to cook completely.

1. Combine broth, beans, tomatoes, zucchini, oil, garlic, dried basil and oregano in **CROCK-POT**® slow cooker; mix well. Cover; cook on LOW 3 to 4 hours.

2. Stir in pasta. Cover; cook on LOW 1 hour or until pasta is tender.

3. Serve soup with croutons and cheese. Garnish with fresh basil.

Recipe courtesy of
Crock-Pot® Slow Cooker Kitchens

Mexican Black Bean and Beef Soup

2 cups water

1 jar (16 ounces) **Pace**® Picante Sauce

1 tablespoon chopped fresh cilantro leaves

1 teaspoon ground cumin

1 large onion, chopped (about 1 cup)

1 cup frozen whole kernel corn

1 can (about 15 ounces) black beans, rinsed and drained

1 pound beef for stew, cut into ½-inch pieces

1. Mix the water, picante sauce, cilantro, cumin, onion, corn, beans and beef in a 3½- to 6-quart **CROCK-POT**® slow cooker.

2. Cover and cook on LOW for 8 to 9 hours* or until the beef is fork-tender.

*Or on HIGH for 4 to 5 hours.

Recipe courtesy of
Campbell's Kitchen

soups

42

French Onion Soup

¼ cup (½ stick) butter

3 pounds yellow onions, sliced

1 tablespoon sugar

2 to 3 tablespoons dry white wine **or** water (optional)

2 quarts (8 cups) **Swanson**® Beef Broth (Regular, 50% Less Sodium **or** Certified Organic)

8 slices French bread (optional)

½ cup (2 ounces) shredded Gruyère **or** Swiss cheese

1. Melt butter in large skillet over medium-low heat. Add onions; cover and cook just until onions are tender and transparent, but not browned, about 10 minutes.

2. Remove cover. Sprinkle sugar over onions. Cook and stir 8 to 10 minutes or until onions are caramelized. Add onions and any browned bits to **CROCK-POT**® slow cooker. If desired, add wine to pan. Bring to a boil, scraping up any browned bits. Add to **CROCK-POT**® slow cooker. Stir in broth. Cover; cook on LOW 8 hours or on HIGH 6 hours.

3. Preheat broiler. To serve, ladle soup into individual soup bowls. If desired, top **each** with **1** or **2** bread slices and **about 1 tablespoon** cheese. Place under broiler until cheese is melted and bubbly.

MAKES 8 SERVINGS

COOK TIME
8 HOURS (LOW) OR
6 HOURS (HIGH)

tip

Substitute 1 cup dry white wine for 1 cup of beef broth.

Recipe courtesy of
Crock-Pot® Slow Cooker Kitchens

Pumpkin Soup with Crumbled Bacon and Toasted Pumpkin Seeds

MAKES 4 SERVINGS

PREP TIME
20 MINUTES

COOK TIME
4 HOURS (HIGH)

44

2 teaspoons olive oil

½ cup raw pumpkin seeds*

3 slices thick-cut bacon

1 medium onion, chopped

1 teaspoon kosher salt

½ teaspoon chipotle chili powder, or more to taste

2 cans (29 ounces *each*) 100% pumpkin purée

4 cups **Swanson**® Chicken Broth (Regular, **Natural Goodness**® *or* Certified Organic)

¾ cup apple cider

½ cup whipping cream *or* half-and-half

Sour cream (optional)

*Raw pumpkin seeds may be found in the produce or ethnic food section of your local supermarket. They may be labeled "pepitas."

1. Spray inside of **CROCK-POT**® slow cooker with cooking spray.

2. In small skillet, heat olive oil over medium-high heat. Add pumpkin seeds to olive oil and stir until seeds begin to pop, about 1 minute. Spoon into small bowl and set aside.

3. Add bacon to skillet and cook until crisp. Remove bacon to paper towels and set aside to cool (do not drain drippings from pan). Reduce heat to medium and add onion to pan. Cook, stirring occasionally, until translucent, about 3 minutes. Stir in salt, chipotle chili powder and black pepper. Transfer to **CROCK-POT**® slow cooker.

4. Whisk pumpkin, chicken broth and apple cider into **CROCK-POT**® slow cooker, whisking until smooth.

5. Cover and cook on HIGH 4 hours. Turn off **CROCK-POT**® slow cooker and remove lid. Whisk in cream and adjust seasoning as necessary. Strain soup into bowls and garnish with pumpkin seeds, cooled bacon (crumbled) and sour cream, if desired.

Recipe courtesy of
Crock-Pot® *Slow Cooker*
Kitchens

Slow-Simmered Chicken Gumbo Ya-Ya

MAKES 8 SERVINGS

PREP TIME
20 MINUTES

COOK TIME
8 HOURS

tip

*You can also stir ½ **pound** of cooked medium shrimp in the **CROCK-POT®** slow cooker during the last 30 minutes of cooking.*

¼ cup all-purpose flour

1 teaspoon dried thyme leaves, crushed

14 skinless, boneless chicken thighs (about 1¾ pounds), cut into 1-inch pieces

2 tablespoons vegetable oil

1 package (16 ounces) smoked sausage, cut into 1-inch pieces

1 can (10¾ ounces) **Campbell's®** Condensed Cream of Celery Soup (Regular *or* 98% Fat Free)

1 can (10½ ounces) **Campbell's®** Condensed Chicken Broth

1 can (14.5 ounces) diced tomatoes

2 teaspoons hot pepper sauce

1 large onion, chopped (about 1 cup)

1 large green pepper, chopped (about 1 cup)

3 stalks celery, sliced (about 1½ cups)

2 bay leaves

1 package (10 ounces) frozen cut okra, thawed

Hot cooked rice (optional)

1. Stir the flour and thyme in a gallon-size resealable plastic bag. Add the chicken and shake to coat.

2. Heat the oil in a 12-inch skillet over medium-high heat. Add the chicken and cook until well browned, stirring often. Remove the chicken from the skillet. Add the sausage to the skillet and cook until well browned, stirring often.

3. Stir the chicken, sausage, soup, broth, tomatoes, hot pepper sauce, onion, green pepper, celery, bay leaves and okra in a 6-quart **CROCK-POT®** slow cooker.

4. Cover and cook on LOW for 8 to 9 hours* or until the chicken is cooked through. Remove and discard the bay leaves. Serve the chicken mixture with the rice, if desired.

*Or on HIGH for 4 to 5 hours.

Recipe courtesy of
Campbell's Kitchen

Albondigas Soup

MAKES 6 SERVINGS

PREP TIME
15 MINUTES

COOK TIME
7 HOURS

4 cups **Swanson**® Beef Broth (Regular, 50% Less Sodium *or* Certified Organic)*

1 jar (11 ounces) **Pace**® Picante Sauce

1 can (about 14.5 ounces) diced tomatoes

3 cloves garlic, minced

¾ cup **uncooked** regular long-grain white rice

Mexican Meatballs

3 tablespoons chopped fresh cilantro leaves

*This recipe is also delicious with Swanson® Chicken Broth (Regular, **Natural Goodness**® or Certified Organic) instead of the beef broth.*

1. Stir the broth, picante sauce, tomatoes, garlic, rice and *Mexican Meatballs* in a 6-quart **CROCK-POT**® slow cooker.

2. Cover and cook on LOW for 7 to 8 hours** or until the rice is tender and the meatballs are cooked through. Sprinkle with the cilantro before serving.

Or on HIGH for 4 to 5 hours.

Mexican Meatballs: Mix thoroughly **1 pound** of ground beef, **1** egg, ⅓ **cup** cornmeal, ⅓ **cup** water, **1 teaspoon** hot pepper sauce and **3 tablespoons** chopped fresh cilantro leaves in a large bowl. Shape the beef mixture firmly into **24** meatballs. Add to the cooker as directed above.

Recipe courtesy of
Campbell's Kitchen

Navy Bean Bacon Chowder

MAKES 6 SERVINGS

COOK TIME
8 TO 9 HOURS (LOW)
PLUS
15 MINUTES (HIGH)

1½ cups dried navy beans

2 cups cold water

6 slices thick-cut bacon

1 medium carrot, cut lengthwise into halves, then cut into 1-inch pieces

1 small turnip, cut into 1-inch pieces

1 stalk celery, chopped

1 medium onion, chopped

1 teaspoon Italian seasoning

⅛ teaspoon black pepper

5¾ cups **Swanson® Natural Goodness®** Chicken Broth

1 cup milk

1. Soak beans overnight in cold water; drain.

2. Cook bacon in medium skillet over medium heat. Drain fat; crumble bacon into **CROCK-POT®** slow cooker. Stir in beans, carrot, turnip, celery, onion, Italian seasoning and pepper. Add broth. Cover; cook on LOW 8 to 9 hours or until beans are tender.

3. Ladle **2 cups** of soup mixture into food processor or blender. Process until smooth; return to **CROCK-POT®** slow cooker. Add milk. Cover; cook on HIGH 15 minutes or until heated through.

Recipe courtesy of
Crock-Pot® Slow Cooker Kitchens

soups

50

Barley and Lentil Soup

soups

52

MAKES 8 SERVINGS

PREP TIME
10 MINUTES

COOK TIME
8 HOURS

Recipe courtesy of
Campbell's Kitchen

8 cups **Swanson**® Beef Broth (Regular, 50% Less Sodium *or* Certified Organic)

2 cloves garlic, minced

1 teaspoon dried oregano leaves, crushed

4 large carrots, sliced (about 3 cups)

1 large onion, chopped (about 1 cup)

½ cup *uncooked* dried lentils

½ cup *uncooked* pearl barley

1. Stir the broth, garlic, oregano, carrots, onion, lentils and barley in a 3½- to 6-quart **CROCK-POT**® slow cooker.

2. Cover and cook on LOW for 8 to 9 hours* or until the lentils and barley are tender.

*Or on HIGH for 4 to 5 hours.

CROCK·POT
· THE ORIGINAL SLOW COOKER ·

Campbell's

Chicken Asopao with Smoked Ham and Manchego Cheese

4 cups **Swanson®** Chicken Broth (Regular, **Natural Goodness®** *or* Certified Organic)

1 teaspoon dried oregano leaves, crushed

1 large onion, chopped (about 1 cup)

1 large green pepper, chopped (about 1 cup)

1 can (about 10 ounces) diced tomatoes with green chilies, undrained

1 pound skinless, boneless chicken thighs, cut into cubes

¾ pound cooked ham, diced

2 cups *uncooked* instant white rice

1 tablespoon drained capers

½ cup grated manchego cheese

1. Stir the broth, oregano, onion, green pepper, tomatoes with chilies, chicken and ham in a 6-quart **CROCK-POT®** slow cooker.

2. Cover and cook on LOW for 7 to 8 hours*.

3. Stir in the rice and capers. Cover and cook for 5 minutes. Sprinkle with the cheese.

Or on HIGH for 4 to 5 hours.

MAKES 8 SERVINGS

PREP TIME
15 MINUTES

COOK TIME
7 HOURS 5 MINUTES

soups

53

tip

If you are unable to find manchego cheese, use Pecorino Romano or Parmesan cheese.

Recipe courtesy of
Campbell's Kitchen

Fennel Soup au Gratin

MAKES 8 SERVINGS

PREP TIME
15 MINUTES

COOK TIME
5 HOURS

8 cups **Swanson®** Beef Broth (Regular, 50% Less Sodium **or** Certified Organic)

2 tablespoons dry sherry

2 teaspoons dried thyme leaves, crushed

3 tablespoons butter

1 bulb fennel, sliced (about 4 cups)

2 large onions, sliced (about 4 cups)

8 slices French bread, about ½-inch thick

½ cup shredded Italian blend cheese (about 2 ounces)

1. Stir the broth, sherry, thyme, butter, fennel and onions in a 5½-quart **CROCK-POT®** slow cooker. Cover and cook on HIGH for 5 to 6 hours or until the vegetables are tender.

2. Heat the broiler. Place the bread slices on a baking sheet. Top **each** bread slice with **1 tablespoon** of the cheese. Broil 4 inches from the heat for 1 minute or until the cheese is melted.

3. Divide the soup mixture among **8** serving bowls. Top **each** with **1** cheese toast.

Recipe courtesy of
Campbell's Kitchen

Yellow Split Pea Soup with Andouille Sausage

MAKES 6 SERVINGS

PREP TIME
15 MINUTES

COOK TIME
4 HOURS

5 cups **Swanson**® Chicken Broth (Regular, **Natural Goodness**® *or* Certified Organic)

3 medium carrots, thinly sliced (about 1½ cups)

3 stalks celery, thinly sliced (about 1½ cups)

1 large red onion, finely chopped (about 1 cup)

¼ cup chopped fresh parsley

4 cloves garlic, chopped

1 bay leaf

2 cups dried yellow split peas

6 ounces andouille sausage, diced (about 1½ cups)

1. Stir the broth, carrots, celery, onion, parsley, garlic, bay leaf, split peas and sausage in a 4-quart **CROCK-POT**® slow cooker.

2. Cover and cook on HIGH for 4 to 5 hours* or until the vegetables are tender. Remove the bay leaf.

3. Place ⅓ of the broth mixture into a blender or food processor. Cover and blend until almost smooth. Pour the mixture into a 3-quart saucepan. Repeat the blending process twice more with the remaining broth mixture. Cook over medium heat until the mixture is hot and bubbling.

Or on LOW for 7 to 8 hours.

Recipe courtesy of
Campbell's Kitchen

Rich and Hearty Drumstick Soup

2 turkey drumsticks (about 1¾ pounds total)

2 medium carrots, peeled and sliced

1 medium stalk celery, thinly sliced

1 cup chopped onion

1 teaspoon minced garlic

½ teaspoon poultry seasoning

4½ cups **Swanson**® Chicken Broth (Regular, **Natural Goodness**® *or* Certified Organic)

2 ounces *uncooked* dry egg noodles

¼ cup chopped parsley

2 tablespoons butter

¾ teaspoon salt, or to taste

1. Coat **CROCK·POT**® slow cooker with nonstick cooking spray. Add drumsticks, carrots, celery, onion, garlic and poultry seasoning. Pour broth over; cover. Cook on HIGH 5 hours or until turkey meat is falling off bones.

2. Remove turkey; set aside. Add noodles to **CROCK·POT**® slow cooker; cover and cook 30 minutes more or until noodles are tender. Meanwhile, debone turkey and cut meat into bite-size pieces; set meat aside.

3. When noodles are cooked, stir in turkey, parsley, butter and salt.

Recipe courtesy of
Crock-Pot® Slow Cooker
Kitchens

soups

Southwestern Chicken & White Bean Soup

MAKES 6 SERVINGS

PREP TIME
15 MINUTES

COOK TIME
8 HOURS

1 tablespoon vegetable oil

1 pound skinless, boneless chicken breasts, cut into 1-inch pieces

1¾ cups **Swanson®** Chicken Broth (Regular, **Natural Goodness®** *or* Certified Organic)

1 cup **Pace®** Picante Sauce

3 cloves garlic, minced

2 teaspoons ground cumin

1 can (about 16 ounces) small white beans, rinsed and drained

1 cup frozen whole kernel corn

1 large onion, chopped (about 1 cup)

1. Heat the oil in a 10-inch skillet over medium-high heat. Add the chicken and cook until it's well browned, stirring often.

2. Stir the chicken, broth, picante sauce, garlic, cumin, beans, corn and onion in a 3½-quart **CROCK-POT®** slow cooker.

3. Cover and cook on LOW for 8 to 9 hours* or until the chicken is cooked through.

Or on HIGH for 4 to 5 hours.

soups

60

Recipe courtesy of
Campbell's Kitchen

Lentil Soup with Beef

3 cans (10½ ounces *each*) **Campbell's®** Condensed French Onion Soup

1 soup can water

3 stalks celery, sliced (about 1½ cups)

3 large carrots, sliced (about 1½ cups)

1½ cups dried lentils

1 can (about 14.5 ounces) diced tomatoes

1 teaspoon dried thyme leaves, crushed

3 cloves garlic, minced

2 pounds beef for stew, cut into 1-inch pieces

1. Stir the soup, water, celery, carrots, lentils, tomatoes, thyme, garlic and beef in a 5-quart **CROCK-POT®** slow cooker. Season as desired.

2. Cover and cook on LOW for 7 to 8 hours* or until the beef is fork-tender.

Or on HIGH for 4 to 5 hours.

Recipe courtesy of
Campbell's Kitchen

soups

62

Persian Split Pea Soup

5 cups **Swanson**® Chicken Broth (Regular, **Natural Goodness**® *or* Certified Organic)

2 pounds beef for stew, cut into 2-inch pieces

3 leeks, cut into 1-inch pieces

1 large onion, chopped (about 1 cup)

1½ cups dried yellow split peas

5 cloves garlic, minced

3 bay leaves

1 teaspoon dried oregano leaves, crushed

2 teaspoons ground cumin

½ cup golden raisins

2 tablespoons lemon juice

1. Stir the broth, beef, leeks, onion, split peas, garlic, bay leaves, oregano, cumin, raisins and lemon juice in a 6-quart **CROCK-POT**® slow cooker.

2. Cover and cook on LOW for 7 to 8 hours or until the beef is fork-tender. Remove the bay leaves.

MAKES 8 SERVINGS

PREP TIME
15 MINUTES

COOK TIME
7 HOURS

soups

63

tip

You can substitute lamb for the beef.

Recipe courtesy of
Campbell's Kitchen

Roast Pork Soup with Soba Noodles and Bok Choy

2 tablespoons hoisin sauce

1 tablespoon sugar

1 to 2 teaspoons Chinese five-spice powder

1 pork loin (about 2½ pounds)

6 cups **Swanson®** Chicken Stock

1½ tablespoons fresh ginger, peeled and cut into thin slices

3 cloves garlic, thinly sliced

2 tablespoons soy sauce

1 head bok choy, sliced

1 pound soba noodles, cooked

1. Preheat oven to 350°F. In small bowl, combine hoisin sauce, sugar and five-spice powder. Baste pork with sauce and roast 45 to 60 minutes, or until just cooked through.

2. Let meat rest 15 minutes and slice into thin matchstick pieces.

3. Place pork in **CROCK-POT®** slow cooker and add stock, ginger, garlic, soy sauce and bok choy. Cover and cook on LOW 6 to 7 hours or on HIGH 3 to 4 hours.

4. Stir in soba noodles and cook until just heated through.

Recipe courtesy of
Crock-Pot® Slow Cooker Kitchens

Russian Borscht

MAKES 12 SERVINGS

COOK TIME
7 TO 9 HOURS (LOW)

4 cups thinly sliced green cabbage

1½ pounds fresh beets, shredded

5 small carrots, halved lengthwise then cut into 1-inch pieces

1 parsnip, peeled, halved lengthwise then cut into 1-inch pieces

1 cup chopped onion

4 cloves garlic, minced

1 pound beef stew meat, cut into ½-inch cubes

1 can (about 14 ounces) diced tomatoes, undrained

3 cans (about 14 ounces *each*) **Swanson**® 50% Less Sodium Beef Broth

¼ cup lemon juice, or more to taste

1 tablespoon sugar, or more to taste

1 teaspoon black pepper

Sour cream (optional)

Fresh parsley (optional)

1. Layer ingredients in **CROCK-POT**® slow cooker in following order: cabbage, beets, carrots, parsnip, onion, garlic, beef, tomatoes, broth, lemon juice, sugar and pepper. Cover; cook on LOW 7 to 9 hours or until vegetables are crisp-tender.

2. Season with additional lemon juice and sugar, if desired. Dollop each serving with sour cream and sprinkle with parsley, if desired.

Recipe courtesy of
Crock-Pot* ***Slow Cooker***
Kitchens

Savory Barley & Tomato Soup

MAKES 6 SERVINGS

PREP TIME
15 MINUTES

COOK TIME
6 HOURS

tip

*Stir in some Swanson®
Chicken Broth or
water to adjust the
consistency, if desired.*

1 can (10¾ ounces) **Campbell's®** Condensed Golden Mushroom Soup

1 can (10½ ounces) **Campbell's®** Condensed Chicken Broth

1 can (about 28 ounces) diced tomatoes

2 soup cans water

2 large onions, diced (about 2 cups)

2 cloves garlic, minced

3 large carrots, diced (about 1½ cups)

½ cup *uncooked* pearl barley

1 teaspoon dried Italian seasoning, crushed

2 tablespoons chopped fresh parsley

1 cup grated Parmesan cheese

Croutons (optional)

1. Stir soup, broth, tomatoes, water, onions, garlic, carrots, barley and Italian seasoning in a 6-quart **CROCK-POT®** slow cooker.

2. Cover and cook on LOW for 6 to 7 hours* or until the barley is tender, stirring once during cooking. Stir in the parsley and cheese. Top with the croutons and additional Parmesan cheese, if desired.

Or on HIGH for 4 to 5 hours.

*Recipe courtesy of
Campbell's Kitchen*

Slow-Simmered Chicken Rice Soup

MAKES 8 SERVINGS

PREP TIME
10 MINUTES

COOK TIME
7 HOURS 15 MINUTES

½ cup *uncooked* wild rice

½ cup *uncooked* regular long-grain white rice

1 tablespoon vegetable oil

5¼ cups **Swanson**® Chicken Broth (Regular, **Natural Goodness**® *or* Certified Organic)

2 teaspoons dried thyme leaves, crushed

¼ teaspoon crushed red pepper

2 stalks celery, coarsely chopped (about 1 cup)

1 medium onion, chopped (about ½ cup)

1 pound skinless, boneless chicken breasts, cut into cubes

Sour cream (optional)

Chopped green onions (optional)

1. Stir the wild rice, white rice and oil in a 3½-quart **CROCK-POT**® slow cooker. Cover and cook on HIGH for 15 minutes.

2. Add the broth, thyme, red pepper, celery, onion and chicken to the **CROCK-POT**® slow cooker. Turn the heat to LOW. Cover and cook for 7 to 8 hours* or until the chicken is cooked through.

3. Serve with the sour cream and green onions, if desired.

Or on HIGH for 4 to 5 hours.

tip

*Speed preparation by substituting **3 cans** (4.5 ounces **each**) **Swanson**® Premium Chunk Chicken Breast, drained, for the raw chicken.*

Recipe courtesy of
Campbell's Kitchen

Thai Coconut Chicken and Rice Soup

1 pound boneless, skinless chicken thighs, cut into 1-inch pieces

3 cups **Swanson® Natural Goodness®** Chicken Broth

1 package (12 ounces) frozen chopped onions

1 can (4 ounces) sliced mushrooms, drained

2 tablespoons minced fresh ginger

2 tablespoons sugar

1 cup cooked rice

1 can (15 ounces) unsweetened coconut milk

½ red bell pepper, seeded and thinly sliced

3 tablespoons chopped fresh cilantro

2 tablespoons grated lime peel

1. Combine chicken, broth, onions, mushrooms, ginger and sugar in **CROCK-POT®** slow cooker. Cover and cook on LOW 8 to 9 hours.

2. Stir rice, coconut milk and red bell pepper into soup. Cover and cook 15 minutes longer. Turn off heat and stir in cilantro and lime peel.

Recipe courtesy of
Crock-Pot® Slow Cooker Kitchens

Creamy Chicken Tortilla Soup

1 cup **Pace®** Picante Sauce

2 cans (10¾ ounces *each*) **Campbell's®** Condensed Cream of Chicken Soup

1 pound skinless, boneless chicken breasts, cut into ½-inch pieces

2 cups frozen whole kernel corn

1 can (about 15 ounces) black beans, rinsed and drained

1 soup can water

1 teaspoon ground cumin

4 corn tortillas (6-inch), cut into strips

1 cup shredded Cheddar cheese (about 4 ounces)

⅓ cup chopped fresh cilantro leaves

MAKES 6 SERVINGS

PREP TIME
15 MINUTES

COOK TIME
4 HOURS 15 MINUTES

1. Stir the picante sauce, soup, chicken, corn, beans, water and cumin in a 4-quart **CROCK-POT®** slow cooker.

2. Cover and cook on LOW for 4 to 5 hours* or until the chicken is cooked through.

3. Stir the tortillas, cheese and cilantro into the **CROCK-POT®** slow cooker. Cover and cook for 15 minutes. Serve with additional cheese, if desired.

Or on HIGH for 2 to 2½ hours.

Recipe courtesy of
Campbell's Kitchen

soups

73

stews, chilis & chowders

Chicken and Vegetable Chowder

MAKES 6 SERVINGS

COOK TIME
5 TO 6 HOURS (LOW)
PLUS
15 MINUTES (HIGH)

1 pound boneless, skinless chicken breasts, cut into 1-inch pieces

1 can (about 14 ounces) **Swanson® Natural Goodness®** Chicken Broth

1 can (10¾ ounces) **Campbell's®** Condensed Cream of Potato Soup, undiluted

1 package (10 ounces) frozen broccoli florets, thawed

1 cup sliced carrots

1 jar (4½ ounces) sliced mushrooms, drained

½ cup chopped onion

½ cup whole kernel corn

2 cloves garlic, minced

½ teaspoon dried thyme leaves

⅓ cup half-and-half

1. Combine chicken, broth, soup, broccoli, carrots, mushrooms, onion, corn, garlic and thyme in **CROCK-POT®** slow cooker; mix well. Cover; cook on LOW 5 to 6 hours.

2. Stir in half-and-half. Cover; cook on HIGH 15 minutes or until heated through.

Variation: Add ½ **cup** (2 ounces) shredded Swiss **or** Cheddar cheese just before serving, stirring over LOW heat until melted.

Recipe courtesy of
Crock-Pot® Slow Cooker Kitchens

Asian Sweet Potato and Corn Stew

MAKES 6 SERVINGS

COOK TIME
5 TO 6 HOURS (LOW)

1 tablespoon vegetable oil

1 large onion, chopped

2 tablespoons peeled and minced fresh ginger

½ jalapeño **or** serrano pepper, seeded and minced*

2 cloves garlic, minced

1 cup drained canned **or** thawed frozen corn kernels

2 teaspoons curry powder

1 can (13½ ounces) coconut milk, well shaken

1 teaspoon cornstarch

1 can (14½ ounces) **Swanson**® Vegetable Broth (Regular **or** Certified Organic)

1 tablespoon soy sauce, plus more to taste

4 sweet potatoes, peeled and cut into ¾-inch cubes

Hot cooked jasmine **or** long grain rice

Chopped cilantro (optional)

*Jalapeño **and** serrano peppers can sting and irritate the skin, so wear rubber gloves when handling peppers and do not touch your eyes.*

1. Heat oil in large skillet over medium heat. Add onion, ginger, minced jalapeño and garlic. Cook, stirring occasionally, until onion softens (about 5 minutes). Remove from heat and stir in drained corn and curry powder.

2. Whisk coconut milk and cornstarch together in **CROCK-POT**® slow cooker. Stir in broth and soy sauce. Carefully add sweet potatoes then top with curried corn. Cover; cook on LOW 5 to 6 hours or until sweet potatoes are tender. Stir gently to smooth cooking liquid (coconut milk may look curdled) without breaking up sweet potatoes. Adjust seasoning to taste with additional soy sauce. Spoon over rice in serving bowls and sprinkle with cilantro, if desired.

Recipe courtesy of
Crock-Pot® Slow Cooker Kitchens

Greek-Style Beef Stew

MAKES 6 SERVINGS

PREP TIME
10 MINUTES

COOK TIME
8 HOURS

1 boneless beef bottom round roast *or* chuck pot roast (about 2 pounds), cut into 1-inch pieces

1 bag (16 ounces) frozen whole small white onions

1 bag (16 ounces) fresh *or* frozen whole baby carrots

2 tablespoons all-purpose flour

1¾ cups **Swanson**® Beef Stock

1 can (5.5 ounces) **V8**® 100% Vegetable Juice

1 tablespoon packed brown sugar

Bouquet Garni

Hot buttered noodles

1. Place the beef, onions and carrots into a 4-quart **CROCK·POT**® slow cooker. Sprinkle with the flour and toss to coat.

2. Stir the stock, vegetable juice and brown sugar in a medium bowl until the mixture is smooth. Pour the stock mixture over the beef and vegetables. Submerge the *Bouquet Garni* into the stock mixture.

3. Cover and cook on LOW for 8 to 9 hours* or until the beef is fork-tender. Remove the *Bouquet Garni*. Serve the beef mixture over the noodles.

Or on HIGH for 4 to 5 hours.

Bouquet Garni: Lay a 4-inch square of cheesecloth flat on the counter. Place ½ **teaspoon** whole cloves, **1** cinnamon stick and **1** bay leaf in the center of the cloth. Bring the corners of the cloth together and tie with kitchen string into a bundle.

Recipe courtesy of
Campbell's Kitchen

Chipotle Chili

MAKES 8 SERVINGS

PREP TIME
15 MINUTES

COOK TIME
8 HOURS

1 jar (16 ounces) **Pace**® Picante Sauce

1 cup water

2 tablespoons chili powder

1 teaspoon ground chipotle chile pepper

1 large onion, chopped (about 1 cup)

2 pounds beef for stew, cut into ½-inch pieces

1 can (about 19 ounces) red kidney beans, rinsed and drained

Shredded Cheddar cheese (optional)

Sour cream (optional)

1. Stir the picante sauce, water, chili powder, chipotle pepper, onion, beef and beans in a 3½-quart **CROCK-POT**® slow cooker.

2. Cover and cook on LOW for 8 to 9 hours* or until the beef is fork-tender. Serve with the cheese and sour cream, if desired.

Or on HIGH for 4 to 5 hours.

Recipe courtesy of
Campbell's Kitchen

Easy Beef Stew

2 pounds beef stew meat, cut into 1-inch cubes

1 can (4 ounces) mushrooms

1 envelope (1 ounce) dry onion soup mix

⅓ cup red *or* white wine

1 can (10¾ ounces) **Campbell's®** Condensed Cream of Mushroom Soup (Regular *or* 98% Fat Free), undiluted

Hot cooked noodles

Combine all ingredients except noodles in **CROCK-POT®** slow cooker. Cover; cook on LOW 8 to 12 hours. Serve over noodles.

MAKES 4 TO 6 SERVINGS

PREP TIME
10 MINUTES

COOK TIME
8 TO 12 HOURS (LOW)

stews, chilis & chowders

81

tip

Browning the beef before cooking it in the CROCK-POT® slow cooker isn't necessary but helps to enhance the flavor and appearance of the stew. If you have the time, use nonstick cooking spray and brown the meat in a large skillet before placing it in the CROCK-POT® slow cooker; follow the recipe as written.

Recipe courtesy of Crock-Pot® Slow Cooker Kitchens

No More "Chili" Nights

MAKES 4 TO 6 SERVINGS

PREP TIME
15 MINUTES

COOK TIME
8 TO 10 HOURS (LOW)

1½ pounds lean ground beef

 1 small onion, chopped

 2 cans (15½ ounces *each*) red kidney beans, drained

 1 can (29 ounces) tomato sauce

 1 can (14½ ounces) diced tomatoes with green peppers, celery and onions, undrained

 1 can (14½ ounces) diced tomatoes and onions, undrained

 1 can water (use 14½-ounce can to measure)

 1 can (10 ounces) diced tomatoes and green chilies, undrained

 ½ green bell pepper, cored, seeded and chopped, plus additional for garnish

 3 tablespoons chili powder

 2 tablespoons sugar

 2 teaspoons salt

 1 teaspoon minced garlic *or* 2 cloves fresh garlic

 1 teaspoon Worcestershire sauce

 1 teaspoon black pepper

 1 teaspoon ground cumin

Shredded cheese (optional)

Pepperidge Farm® Assorted Crackers (optional)

1. Brown ground beef and onion 6 to 8 minutes in large skillet over medium-high heat, stirring to break up meat. Drain and discard excess fat. Transfer meat mixture to **CROCK-POT**® slow cooker.

2. Add remaining ingredients. Stir well to combine. Cover; cook on LOW 8 to 10 hours. Garnish with cheese and bell pepper; serve with crackers, if desired.

Recipe courtesy of
Crock-Pot® Slow Cooker
Kitchens

Slow Cooker Beef & Mushroom Stew

MAKES 6 SERVINGS

PREP TIME
20 MINUTES

COOK TIME
10 HOURS 15 MINUTES

1 boneless beef bottom round roast **or** chuck pot roast (about 1½ pounds), cut into 1-inch pieces

Ground black pepper

¼ cup all-purpose flour

2 tablespoons vegetable oil

1 can (10½ ounces) **Campbell's®** Condensed French Onion Soup

1 cup Burgundy **or** other dry red wine

2 cloves garlic, minced

1 teaspoon Italian seasoning, crushed

10 ounces mushrooms, cut in half (about 3 cups)

3 medium carrots, cut into 2-inch pieces (about 1½ cups)

1 cup frozen whole small white onions

¼ cup water

1. Season the beef with the black pepper. Coat the beef with **2 tablespoons** flour. Heat the oil in a 12-inch skillet over medium-high heat. Add the beef and cook until it's well browned, stirring often.

2. Stir the beef, soup, wine, garlic, Italian seasoning, mushrooms, carrots and onions in a 3½-quart **CROCK-POT®** slow cooker.

3. Cover and cook on LOW for 10 to 11 hours* or until the beef is fork-tender.

4. Stir the remaining flour and water in a small bowl until the mixture is smooth. Stir the flour mixture in the **CROCK-POT®** slow cooker. Increase the heat to HIGH. Cover and cook for 15 minutes or until the mixture boils and thickens.

Or on HIGH for 5 to 6 hours.

Recipe courtesy of
Campbell's Kitchen

Wild Mushroom Beef Stew

MAKES 5 SERVINGS

PREP TIME
15 TO 20 MINUTES

COOK TIME
10 TO 12 HOURS (LOW)
OR 4 HOURS (HIGH)

1½ to 2 pounds beef stew meat, cut into 1-inch cubes

2 tablespoons all-purpose flour

½ teaspoon salt

½ teaspoon black pepper

1½ cups **Swanson®** Beef Broth (Regular, 50% Less Sodium **or** Certified Organic)

1 teaspoon Worcestershire sauce

1 clove garlic, minced

1 bay leaf

1 teaspoon paprika

4 shiitake mushrooms, sliced

2 medium carrots, sliced

2 medium potatoes, diced

1 small white onion, chopped

1 stalk celery, sliced

tip

You may double the amount of meat, mushrooms, carrots, potatoes, onion and celery for a 5-, 6- or 7-quart CROCK-POT® slow cooker.

1. Put beef in **CROCK-POT®** slow cooker. Mix together flour, salt and pepper and sprinkle over meat; stir to coat each piece of meat with flour. Add remaining ingredients and stir to mix well.

2. Cover; cook on LOW 10 to 12 hours or on HIGH 4 to 6 hours. Stir stew before serving.

Note: This classic beef stew is given a twist with the addition of flavorful shiitake mushrooms. If shiitake mushrooms are unavailable in your local grocery store, you can substitute other mushrooms of your choice. For extra punch, add a few dried porcini mushrooms to the stew.

Recipe courtesy of
Crock-Pot® Slow Cooker Kitchens

Hearty Mixed Bean Stew with Sausage

MAKES 8 SERVINGS

PREP TIME
15 MINUTES

COOK TIME
8 HOURS

¾ pound sweet Italian pork sausage, casing removed

10 cups **Swanson**® Chicken Stock

¼ teaspoon ground black pepper

2 medium carrots, chopped (about ⅔ cup)

1 stalk celery, chopped (about ½ cup)

4 ounces dried pinto beans (about ¾ cup)

4 ounces dried navy beans (about ¾ cup)

4 ounces dried kidney beans (about ¾ cup)

6 sun-dried tomatoes in oil, drained and thinly sliced (about ¼ cup)

Grated Parmesan cheese

1. Cook the sausage in a 10-inch skillet over medium-high heat until it's well browned, stirring often to separate the meat. Pour off any fat.

2. Stir the sausage, stock, black pepper, carrots, celery and beans in a 5-quart **CROCK-POT**® slow cooker.

3. Cover and cook on LOW for 7 to 8 hours.*

4. Stir in the tomatoes. Cover and cook for 1 hour or until the beans are tender. Sprinkle with the cheese.

Or on HIGH for 4 to 5 hours.

Recipe courtesy of
Campbell's Kitchen

Bacon Potato Chowder

4 slices bacon, cooked and crumbled

1 large onion, chopped (about 1 cup)

4 cans (10¾ ounces *each*) Campbell's® Condensed Cream of Potato Soup

4 soup cans milk

¼ teaspoon ground black pepper

2 large russet potatoes, cut into ½-inch pieces (about 3 cups)

½ cup chopped fresh chives

2 cups shredded Cheddar cheese (about 8 ounces)

1. Stir the bacon, onion, soup, milk, black pepper, potatoes and ¼ **cup** chives in a 6-quart **CROCK-POT**® slow cooker.

2. Cover and cook on HIGH for 3 to 4 hours or until the potatoes are tender.

3. Add the cheese and stir until the cheese is melted. Serve with the remaining chives.

MAKES 8 SERVINGS

PREP TIME
15 MINUTES

COOK TIME
3 HOURS

stews, chilis & chowders

89

Recipe courtesy of
Campbell's Kitchen

West African Chicken Stew

MAKES 6 SERVINGS

PREP TIME
5 MINUTES

COOK TIME
7 HOURS

½ cup all-purpose flour

2 teaspoons pumpkin pie spice

1 teaspoon paprika

½ teaspoon cracked black pepper

6 bone-in chicken thighs

6 chicken drumsticks

2 tablespoons vegetable oil

1 can (10¾ ounces) **Campbell's**® Condensed French Onion Soup

½ cup water

1 cup raisins*

½ cup orange juice

1 teaspoon grated orange peel

2 tablespoons chopped fresh parsley **or** cilantro leaves

6 cups hot cooked couscous

*You may substitute chopped prunes **or** apricots for the raisins, if you like.*

1. Mix the flour, pumpkin pie spice, paprika and black pepper on a plate. Coat the chicken with the flour mixture.

2. Heat the oil in a 12-inch skillet over medium heat. Add the chicken and cook for 10 minutes or until it's well browned.

3. Stir the soup, water, raisins, orange juice and orange peel in a 6-quart **CROCK-POT**® slow cooker. Add the chicken and turn to coat.

4. Cover and cook on LOW for 7 to 8 hours** or until the chicken is cooked through.

5. Stir the parsley into the **CROCK-POT**® slow cooker. Serve with the couscous.

**Or on HIGH for 4 to 5 hours.

Recipe courtesy of
Campbell's Kitchen

Stew Provençal

MAKES 8 SERVINGS

COOK TIME
8 TO 10 HOURS (LOW)
OR
4 TO 5 HOURS (HIGH)

2 cans (14½ ounces *each*) **Swanson**® Beef Broth (Regular, 50% Less Sodium *or* Certified Organic), divided

⅓ cup all-purpose flour

1 to 2 pork tenderloins (about 2 pounds), trimmed and diced

4 red potatoes, unpeeled, cut into cubes

2 cups frozen cut green beans, thawed

1 onion, chopped

2 cloves garlic, minced

1 teaspoon salt

1 teaspoon dried thyme

½ teaspoon black pepper

1. Combine ¾ **cup** beef broth and flour in small bowl. Cover and refrigerate.

2. Add remaining broth, pork, potatoes, beans, onion, garlic, salt, thyme and pepper to **CROCK-POT**® slow cooker; mix well.

3. Cover; cook on LOW 8 to 10 hours or on HIGH 4 to 5 hours. Stir flour mixture into **CROCK-POT**® slow cooker. Cook, uncovered, 30 minutes or until thickened.

Recipe courtesy of
Crock-Pot® Slow Cooker Kitchens

Spicy Verde Chicken & Bean Chili

MAKES 6 SERVINGS

PREP TIME
10 MINUTES

COOK TIME
2 HOURS 15 MINUTES

2 tablespoons butter

1 large onion, chopped (about 1 cup)

¼ teaspoon garlic powder **or** 2 cloves garlic

2 cups **Swanson**® Chicken Stock

2 cups shredded cooked chicken

1 can (about 15 ounces) small white beans, undrained

1 can (about 4 ounces) diced green chiles, drained

1 teaspoon ground cumin

1 teaspoon jalapeño hot pepper sauce

1 tablespoon all-purpose flour

1 tablespoon water

6 flour tortillas (8-inch), warmed

Shredded Monterey Jack cheese (optional)

Chopped fresh cilantro leaves (optional)

1. Heat the butter in a 12-inch skillet over medium heat. Add the onion and garlic powder and cook until the onion is tender, stirring occasionally.

2. Stir the onion, stock, chicken, beans, chiles, cumin and hot pepper sauce in a 5-quart **CROCK-POT**® slow cooker. Cover and cook on HIGH for 2 hours.

3. Stir the flour and water in a small cup until the mixture is smooth. Stir the flour mixture in the **CROCK-POT**® slow cooker. Cover and cook for 15 minutes or until the mixture boils and thickens.

4. Place the tortillas into **6** serving bowls. Divide the chili among the bowls. Top with the cheese and cilantro, if desired.

Recipe courtesy of
Campbell's Kitchen

Easy Chili

MAKES 4 SERVINGS

COOK TIME
6 HOURS (LOW)

1 teaspoon vegetable oil

1 pound 95% lean ground beef

1 medium onion, chopped

2 cans (10¾ ounces *each*) **Campbell's**® Condensed Tomato Soup, undiluted

1 cup water

Salt *and* black pepper

Chili powder

1. Heat oil in large skillet over medium-high heat. Add beef and onion. Cook and stir until beef is well browned. Drain excess fat.

2. Place meat mixture, soup and water in **CROCK-POT**® slow cooker. Add salt, pepper and chili powder, to taste. Cover; cook on LOW 6 hours.

tip

This dish can cook up to 8 hours. Garnish with shredded cheese and serve with crackers or thick slices of Italian bread.

Recipe courtesy of
Crock-Pot® Slow Cooker Kitchens

Lentil Stew over Couscous

3 cups dried lentils (1 pound), sorted and rinsed

3 cups water

1 can (about 14 ounces) **Swanson® Natural Goodness®** Chicken Broth

1 can (about 14 ounces) diced tomatoes

1 large onion, chopped

1 green bell pepper, chopped

4 stalks celery, chopped

1 medium carrot, halve lengthwise and sliced

2 cloves garlic, chopped

1 teaspoon dried marjoram

¼ teaspoon black pepper

1 tablespoon olive oil

1 tablespoon cider vinegar

4½ to 5 cups hot cooked couscous

1. Combine lentils, water, broth, tomatoes, onion, bell pepper, celery, carrot, garlic, marjoram and black pepper in **CROCK-POT®** slow cooker; stir. Cover and cook on LOW 8 to 9 hours or until vegetables are tender.

2. Stir in oil and vinegar. Serve over couscous.

MAKES 12 SERVINGS

PREP TIME
10 MINUTES

COOK TIME
8 TO 9 HOURS (LOW)

stews, chilis & chowders

tip

Lentil stew keeps well in the refrigerator for up to 1 week. Stew can also be frozen in an airtight container for up to 3 months.

Recipe courtesy of
Crock-Pot® Slow Cooker Kitchens

Veal Stew with Garden Vegetables

MAKES 6 SERVINGS

PREP TIME
25 MINUTES

COOK TIME
8 HOURS

tips

You can substitute skinless, boneless chicken thighs for the veal.

*For more flavorful rice **or** barley, cook it in **Swanson**® Chicken Broth.*

2 to 2½ pounds veal for stew, cut into 1-inch pieces

Ground black pepper

2 tablespoons olive oil

1 bag (16 ounces) fresh **or** thawed frozen whole baby carrots

1 large onion, diced (about 1 cup)

5 cloves garlic, minced

¼ cup all-purpose flour

2 cups **Swanson**® Chicken Stock

½ teaspoon dried rosemary leaves, crushed

1 can (14.5 ounces) diced tomatoes

1 cup frozen peas, thawed

Hot cooked rice **or** barley

1. Season the veal with the black pepper.

2. Heat the oil in a 12-inch skillet over medium-high heat. Add the veal in 2 batches and cook until it's well browned, stirring often.

3. Place the veal, carrots, onion and garlic into a 4-quart **CROCK-POT**® slow cooker. Sprinkle with the flour and toss to coat.

4. Stir in the stock, rosemary and tomatoes. Cover and cook on LOW for 7 to 8 hours*.

5. Add the peas to the **CROCK-POT**® slow cooker. Cover and cook for 1 hour or until the veal is fork-tender. Season with additional black pepper. Serve the veal mixture with the rice.

Or on HIGH for 4 to 5 hours.

Recipe courtesy of
Campbell's Kitchen

Black Bean and Turkey Stew

MAKES 6 SERVINGS

COOK TIME
6 TO 8 HOURS (LOW)

3 cans (15 ounces *each*) black beans, rinsed and drained

1½ cups chopped onions

1½ cups **Swanson® Natural Goodness®** Chicken Broth

1 cup sliced celery

1 cup chopped red bell pepper

4 cloves garlic, minced

1½ teaspoons dried oregano leaves

¾ teaspoon ground coriander

½ teaspoon ground cumin

¼ teaspoon ground red pepper

6 ounces cooked turkey sausage, thinly sliced

1. Combine all ingredients except sausage in **CROCK-POT®** slow cooker. Cover; cook on LOW 6 to 8 hours.

2. Transfer about 1½ cups bean mixture from **CROCK-POT®** slow cooker to blender or food processor; purée bean mixture. Return to **CROCK-POT®** slow cooker. Stir in sausage. Cover; cook on LOW an additional 10 to 15 minutes.

Recipe courtesy of
Crock-Pot® Slow Cooker Kitchens

Slow Cooker Tuscan Beef Stew

MAKES 8 SERVINGS

PREP TIME
15 MINUTES

COOK TIME
8 HOURS 10 MINUTES

1 can (10¾ ounces) **Campbell's®** Condensed Tomato Soup

1 can (10½ ounces) **Campbell's®** Condensed Beef Broth

½ cup Burgundy wine *or* other dry red wine *or* water

1 teaspoon dried Italian seasoning, crushed

½ teaspoon garlic powder

1 can (14.5 ounces) diced tomatoes with Italian herbs

3 large carrots, cut into 1-inch pieces (about 2 cups)

2 pounds beef for stew, cut into 1-inch pieces

2 cans (about 15 ounces *each*) white kidney beans (cannellini), rinsed and drained

1. Stir the soup, broth, wine, Italian seasoning, garlic powder, tomatoes, carrots and beef in a 3½-quart **CROCK-POT®** slow cooker.

2. Cover and cook on LOW for 8 to 9 hours* or until the beef is fork-tender.

3. Stir in the beans. Increase the heat to HIGH. Cook for 10 minutes or until the mixture is hot.

Or on HIGH for 4 to 5 hours.

Recipe courtesy of
Campbell's Kitchen

Slow-Cooked Panama Pork Stew

MAKES 8 SERVINGS

PREP TIME
20 MINUTES

COOK TIME
7 HOURS

2 cups **Swanson®** Chicken Broth (Regular, **Natural Goodness®** *or* Certified Organic)

4 medium sweet potatoes, peeled and cut into 2-inch pieces

2 medium green peppers, cut into 1-inch pieces (about 2 cups)

1½ cups frozen whole kernel corn, thawed

1 large onion, chopped (about 1 cup)

4 cloves garlic, minced

1 can (about 14.5 ounces) diced tomatoes with green chiles

¼ cup chopped fresh cilantro leaves

1 teaspoon chili powder

2 pounds boneless pork shoulder, cut into 1-inch pieces

1. Stir the broth, sweet potatoes, peppers, corn, onion, garlic, tomatoes, cilantro, chili powder and pork in a 4½- to 5-quart **CROCK-POT®** slow cooker.

2. Cover and cook on LOW for 7 to 8 hours* or until the pork is fork-tender.

Or on HIGH for 4 to 5 hours.

Recipe courtesy of
Campbell's Kitchen

beef main dishes

Bistro-Style Short Ribs

MAKES 4 SERVINGS

PREP TIME
10 MINUTES

COOK TIME
1 HOUR 45 MINUTES

Vegetable cooking spray

3 pounds beef short ribs, cut into individual rib pieces

1 large onion, chopped (about 1 cup)

2 medium carrots, chopped (about ⅔ cup)

1 stalk celery, chopped (about ½ cup)

2¾ cups **Prego**® Traditional *or* Marinara Italian Sauce

1¾ cups **Swanson**® Beef Stock

1. Spray a 6-quart oven-safe saucepot with the cooking spray and heat over medium-high heat for 1 minute. Add the ribs in 2 batches and cook until they're browned on all sides. Remove the ribs from the saucepot. Pour off all but **2 tablespoons** fat.

2. Add the onion, carrots and celery to the saucepot and cook until they're tender. Stir the Italian sauce and stock in the saucepot and heat to a boil. Return the ribs to the saucepot. Cover the saucepot.

3. Bake at 350°F. for 1 hour 30 minutes or until the ribs are fork-tender.

For Slow-Cooked Bistro-Style Ribs: Brown the ribs in a 12-inch skillet as directed in step 1. Place the onion, carrots and celery in a 5-quart **CROCK-POT**® slow cooker. Top with the ribs. Pour the Italian sauce and stock in the **CROCK-POT**® slow cooker. Cover and cook on LOW for 7 to 8 hours* or until the ribs are fork-tender.

Or on HIGH for 3½ to 4 hours.

Recipe courtesy of
Campbell's Kitchen

Portuguese Madeira Beef Shanks

MAKES 4 SERVINGS

PREP TIME
15 MINUTES

COOK TIME
7 TO 9 HOURS (LOW)

4 cloves garlic, minced

1 large white onion, diced

1 green bell pepper, cored and diced

2 jalapeño peppers, seeded and minced*

½ cup diced celery

½ cup minced parsley

4 medium beef shanks, bone in (about 3 pounds total)

1 tablespoon fresh rosemary leaves, minced

1 teaspoon salt

1 cup **Swanson®** Beef Broth (Regular, 50% Less Sodium **or** Certified Organic)

1 cup dry Madeira wine

4 cups hot cooked rice

Horseradish sauce (optional)

Jalapeño peppers can sting and irritate the skin, so wear rubber gloves when handling peppers and do not touch your eyes.

1. Place garlic, onion, bell pepper, jalapeño peppers, celery and parsley in **CROCK-POT®** slow cooker.

2. Rub beef shanks with rosemary and salt. Place shanks on top of vegetables. Pour broth and wine over shanks and vegetables. Cover; cook on LOW 7 to 9 hours.

3. To serve, spoon **1 cup** rice into each soup plate. Top rice with beef shank. Spoon vegetable sauce over shanks. Serve with horseradish sauce, if desired.

Recipe courtesy of
Crock-Pot® Slow Cooker Kitchens

Slow Cooker Cassoulet

MAKES 4 SERVINGS

PREP TIME
30 MINUTES

COOK TIME
8 HOURS (LOW)

1 pound white beans, such as Great Northern

Boiling water to cover beans

1 tablespoon butter

1 tablespoon canola oil

4 veal shanks, 1½ inches thick, tied for cooking

3 cups **Swanson**® Beef Broth (Regular, 50% Less Sodium **or** Certified Organic)

4 ounces maple-smoked bacon **or** pancetta, diced

3 cloves garlic, smashed

1 sprig **each** thyme **and** savory **or** 1 tablespoon **each** dried thyme **and** dried savory

2 whole cloves

Salt **and** black pepper, to taste

4 links mild Italian sausages

1. Rinse and sort beans and place in large bowl; cover completely with water. Soak 6 to 8 hours or overnight. Drain beans; discard water.

2. Heat butter and oil in large skillet over medium-high heat until hot. Sear shanks on all sides until browned. Transfer to **CROCK-POT**® slow cooker. Add broth, bacon, garlic, beans, herbs and cloves. Add enough water to cover beans, if needed. Cover; cook on LOW 8 hours. After 4 hours, check liquid and add boiling water as needed to barely cover beans.

3. Before serving, season with salt and pepper. Grill sausages; serve with cassoulet.

Quick-soak beans: To quick-soak beans, place beans in large saucepan; cover with water. Bring to a boil over high heat. Boil 2 minutes. Remove from heat; let soak, covered, 1 hour.

Recipe courtesy of
Crock-Pot® Slow Cooker
Kitchens

Asian Ginger Beef over Bok Choy

MAKES 6 TO 8 SERVINGS

PREP TIME
15 MINUTES

COOK TIME
7 TO 8 HOURS (LOW)
OR
3 TO 4 HOURS (HIGH)

2 tablespoons peanut oil

1½ pounds boneless beef chuck roast, cut into 1-inch pieces

3 green onions, cut into ½-inch slices

6 cloves garlic

1 cup **Swanson**® Chicken Broth (Regular, **Natural Goodness**® *or* Certified Organic)

½ cup water

¼ cup soy sauce

2 teaspoons ground ginger

1 teaspoon Asian chili paste

9 ounces fresh udon noodles *or* vermicelli, cooked and drained

3 cups bok choy, trimmed, washed and cut into 1-inch pieces

½ cup minced fresh cilantro

1. Heat oil in large skillet over medium-high heat until hot. Sear beef on all sides in batches to prevent crowding, turning each piece as it browns. Sear last batch of beef with onions and garlic.

2. Transfer to **CROCK-POT**® slow cooker. Add broth, water, soy sauce, ginger and chili paste. Stir well to combine. Cover; cook on LOW 7 to 8 hours or on HIGH 3 to 4 hours, or until beef is very tender.

3. Just before serving, turn **CROCK-POT**® slow cooker to HIGH. Add noodles to **CROCK-POT**® slow cooker and stir well. Add bok choy and stir again. Cook on HIGH until bok choy is tender-crisp, about 15 minutes.

4. Garnish beef with cilantro and serve while hot.

Recipe courtesy of
Crock-Pot® Slow Cooker Kitchens

Slow-Simmered Pot Roast with Garden Vegetables

MAKES 6 SERVINGS

PREP TIME
15 MINUTES

COOK TIME
10 HOURS

4 medium potatoes, cut into quarters (about 4 cups)

2 cups fresh *or* frozen whole baby carrots

2 stalks celery, cut into 1-inch pieces (about 1½ cups)

1 beef bottom round roast, trimmed of all fat (about 2 pounds)

½ teaspoon ground black pepper

1 carton (18.3 ounces) **Campbell's® V8®** Butternut Squash Soup

1 tablespoon minced garlic

Fresh parsley

1. Place the potatoes, carrots and celery into a 4- to 6-quart **CROCK-POT®** slow cooker. Season the beef with the black pepper and place on the vegetables.

2. Add the soup and garlic and toss to coat.

3. Cover and cook on LOW for 10 to 11 hours or until the beef is fork-tender. Garnish with parsley, if desired.

tip

*For thicker gravy, stir ¼ **cup** all-purpose flour and ½ **cup** water in a small bowl until it's smooth. Remove the beef from the **CROCK-POT®** slow cooker. Stir in the flour mixture. Cover and cook on HIGH for 10 minutes or until the mixture boils and thickens.*

*Recipe courtesy of **Campbell's Kitchen***

Burgundy and Wild Cremini Mushroom Pilaf

2 tablespoons vegetable oil

2 cups converted long grain white rice

1 medium onion, chopped

1 cup sliced wild cremini mushrooms

1 small zucchini, thinly sliced

3½ cups **Swanson**® Beef Broth (Regular, 50% Less Sodium **or** Certified Organic) **or** Vegetable Broth (Regular **or** Certified Organic)

½ cup burgundy **or** other red wine

½ teaspoon salt

¼ teaspoon black pepper

4 tablespoons (½ stick) butter, melted

MAKES 6 SERVINGS

PREP TIME
15 MINUTES

COOK TIME
6 TO 8 HOURS (LOW)

beef main dishes

1. Heat oil in skillet over medium heat until hot. Add rice, onion, mushrooms and zucchini. Cook and stir 4 to 5 minutes until rice is slightly browned and onions are soft. Transfer to **CROCK-POT**® slow cooker.

2. Add broth, burgundy, salt and pepper. Drizzle melted butter over all. Stir once. Cover; cook on LOW 6 to 8 hours.

Recipe courtesy of
Crock-Pot® Slow Cooker Kitchens

Creamy Beef Stroganoff

MAKES 9 SERVINGS

PREP TIME
15 MINUTES

COOK TIME
8 HOURS

2 cans (10¾ ounces *each*) **Campbell's**® Condensed Cream of Mushroom Soup

¼ cup water

2 tablespoons Worcestershire sauce

1 package (8 ounces) sliced white mushrooms

3 medium onions, coarsely chopped (about 1½ cups)

3 cloves garlic, minced

½ teaspoon ground black pepper

2 pounds boneless beef bottom round steaks, sliced diagonally into strips

1 cup sour cream

Hot cooked egg noodles

Chopped fresh parsley (optional)

tip

For more overall flavor and color, brown the beef before adding it to the CROCK-POT® slow cooker.

1. Stir the soup, water, Worcestershire sauce, mushrooms, onions, garlic and black pepper in a 6-quart **CROCK-POT**® slow cooker. Add the beef and stir to coat.

2. Cover and cook on LOW for 8 to 9 hours* or until the beef is cooked through.

3. Stir the sour cream into the cooker. Serve with the egg noodles. Top with the parsley, if desired.

Or on HIGH for 4 to 5 hours.

Recipe courtesy of
Campbell's Kitchen

Slow-Cooked Corned Beef & Cabbage

3½ cups **Swanson®** Beef Stock

¼ cup cider vinegar

2 medium onions, cut into quarters

5 medium potatoes, peeled and cut into quarters (about 5 cups)

5 medium carrots, cut into 2-inch pieces (about 2½ cups)

1 corned beef **or** beef brisket (about 3 pounds)

1 head green cabbage, trimmed and cut into 6 wedges (about 2 pounds)

Bouquet Garni

1. Stir the stock and vinegar into a 6-quart **CROCK-POT®** slow cooker. Add the onions, potatoes, carrots, beef and cabbage. Submerge the Bouquet Garni in the broth mixture.

2. Cover and cook on LOW for 8 to 9 hours* or until the beef is fork-tender. Remove the Bouquet Garni.

*Or on HIGH for 4 to 5 hours.

Bouquet Garni: Lay a 4-inch square of cheesecloth flat on the counter. Place **4** cloves garlic, **1 tablespoon** pickling spice and **2** bay leaves in the center of the cloth. Bring the corners of the cheesecloth together and tie with kitchen string into a bundle.

MAKES 10 SERVINGS

PREP TIME
20 MINUTES

COOK TIME
8 HOURS

tip

For a thicker sauce: Remove the beef and vegetables from the CROCK-POT® slow cooker. Stir 2 tablespoons cornstarch and 2 tablespoons water in a small bowl until smooth. Add to the CROCK-POT® slow cooker and cook on HIGH for 15 minutes or until the mixture boils and thickens.

Recipe courtesy of Campbell's Kitchen

Sauvignon Blanc Beef with Beets and Thyme

MAKES 6 SERVINGS

COOK TIME
8 TO 10 HOURS (LOW)

1 pound red *or* yellow beets, scrubbed and quartered

2 tablespoons extra-virgin olive oil

1 beef chuck roast (about 3 pounds)

1 medium yellow onion, peeled and quartered

2 cloves garlic, minced

5 sprigs fresh thyme

1 whole bay leaf

2 whole cloves

1 cup **Swanson**® Chicken Broth (Regular, **Natural Goodness**® *or* Certified Organic)

1 cup Sauvignon Blanc *or* other white wine

2 tablespoons tomato paste

Salt *and* black pepper, to taste

1. Layer beets evenly in **CROCK-POT**® slow cooker.

2. Heat oil in large skillet over medium heat until hot. Sear roast on all sides 4 to 5 minutes, turning as it browns. Add onion and garlic during last few minutes of searing. Transfer to **CROCK-POT**® slow cooker.

3. Add thyme, bay leaf and cloves. Combine broth, wine and tomato paste in medium bowl. Add salt and pepper. Mix well to combine. Pour over roast and beets. Cover; cook on LOW 8 to 10 hours, or until roast is fork-tender and beets are tender.

Recipe courtesy of
Crock-Pot® Slow Cooker Kitchens

Sauerbraten

MAKES 6 SERVINGS

PREP TIME
15 MINUTES

MARINATE TIME
72 HOURS

COOK TIME
7 HOURS

2	cups cider vinegar
1	cup packed dark brown sugar
2	large onions, sliced (about 2 cups)
2	large carrots, cut into 2-inch pieces (about 1 cup)
10	gingersnap cookies, crushed
1	can (10½ ounces) **Campbell's®** Condensed Beef Consommé *Bouquet Garni*
1	cup water
	4- to 5 -pound boneless beef rump roast
2	tablespoons vegetable oil
1	cup Burgundy wine
½	cup golden raisins
½	cup sour cream (optional)

1. Heat the vinegar, brown sugar, onions, carrots, gingersnaps, consommé and *Bouquet Garni* in a 2-quart saucepan over medium-high heat to a boil. Remove from the heat. Stir in the water and let cool to room temperature.

2. Place the beef in a large nonmetallic bowl. Add the vinegar mixture and turn to coat. Cover and refrigerate for about 72 hours, turning the beef over in the marinade 1 to 2 times per day.

3. Remove the beef from the bowl and pat dry with paper towels. Reserve the marinade mixture.

4. Heat the oil in a 12-inch skillet over medium-high heat. Add the beef and cook until it's well browned on all sides. Remove the beef from the skillet and place it into a 6-quart **CROCK-POT®** slow cooker.

5. Add the wine to the skillet and heat to a boil, stirring often. Pour the wine and reserved marinade over the beef.

6. Cover and cook on LOW for 7 to 8 hours* or until the beef is fork-tender. Stir in the raisins and the sour cream, if desired.

Or on HIGH for 4 to 5 hours.

tip

For a thicker sauce: Before adding the raisins and sour cream, remove the beef from the CROCK-POT® slow cooker. Stir 2 tablespoons cornstarch and 1 cup sauce from the slow cooker in a small bowl. Stir into the CROCK-POT® slow cooker. Turn the heat to HIGH. Cover and cook for 15 minutes or until the mixture boils and thickens.

Bouquet Garni: Lay a 4-inch square of cheesecloth flat on the counter. Place ⅓ **cup** of pickling spice in the center of the cloth. Bring the corners of the cloth together and tie with kitchen string into a bundle.

Recipe courtesy of
Campbell's Kitchen

Slow-Cooked Taco Shredded Beef

MAKES 16 SERVINGS

PREP TIME
10 MINUTES

COOK TIME
6 HOURS 10 MINUTES

1 can (10¾ ounces) **Campbell's®** Condensed French Onion Soup

1 tablespoon chili powder

½ teaspoon ground cumin

   2-pound boneless beef chuck roast

2 tablespoons finely chopped fresh cilantro leaves

16 taco shells

1 cup shredded Cheddar cheese (about 4 ounces)

   Shredded lettuce

   Sour cream

1. Stir the soup, chili powder and cumin in a 4-quart **CROCK-POT®** slow cooker. Add the beef and turn to coat.

2. Cover and cook on LOW for 6 to 7 hours* or until the beef is fork-tender.

3. Remove the beef from the **CROCK-POT®** slow cooker to a cutting board and let stand for 10 minutes. Using 2 forks, shred the beef. Return the beef to the **CROCK-POT®** slow cooker. Stir the cilantro in the slow cooker.

4. Spoon **about ¼ cup** beef mixture into **each** taco shell. Top **each** with **about 1 tablespoon** cheese. Top with the lettuce and the sour cream.

Or on HIGH for 4 to 5 hours.

Recipe courtesy of
Campbell's Kitchen

Sloppy Sloppy Joes

MAKES 20 TO 25 SERVINGS

COOK TIME
4 TO 6 HOURS (LOW)

4 pounds ground beef

1 cup chopped onion

1 cup chopped green bell pepper

1 can (about 28 ounces) tomato sauce

2 cans (10¾ ounces each) **Campbell's®** Condensed Tomato Soup, undiluted

1 cup packed brown sugar

¼ cup ketchup

3 tablespoons Worcestershire sauce

1 tablespoon ground mustard

1 tablespoon prepared mustard

1½ teaspoons chili powder

1 teaspoon garlic powder

Toasted hamburger buns

1. Brown beef in large skillet over medium-high heat, stirring to break up meat. Drain and discard fat.

2. Add onion and bell pepper; cook and stir 5 to 10 minutes or until onion is translucent and mixture is fragrant.

3. Transfer mixture to **CROCK-POT®** slow cooker. Add remaining ingredients except buns; stir until well blended. Cover; cook on LOW 4 to 6 hours. Serve on buns.

Recipe courtesy of
Crock-Pot® Slow Cooker Kitchens

Balsamic Beef with Mushrooms

MAKES 6 SERVINGS

PREP TIME
15 MINUTES

COOK TIME
7 HOURS

Vegetable cooking spray

2 pounds boneless beef chuck roasts, 1-inch thick

2⅔ cups **Prego®** Traditional Italian Sauce

⅓ cup balsamic vinegar

2 packages (8 ounces **each**) sliced mushrooms

1 slice bacon, cooked and crumbled

Hot cooked egg noodles

1. Spray a 10-inch skillet with the cooking spray and heat over medium-high heat for 1 minute. Add the beef and cook until it's well browned on both sides.

2. Stir the Italian sauce, vinegar, mushrooms and bacon in a 5-quart **CROCK-POT®** slow cooker. Add the beef and turn to coat.

3. Cover and cook on LOW for 7 to 8 hours* or until the beef is fork-tender. Serve with the egg noodles.

Or on HIGH for 4 to 5 hours.

Recipe courtesy of
Campbell's Kitchen

CROCK·POT®
·THE ORIGINAL SLOW COOKER·

Campbell's

Spiced Pot Roast

4-pound boneless beef bottom round roast **or** chuck pot roast

4 cloves garlic, peeled

1 tablespoon chili powder

½ teaspoon ground coriander

½ teaspoon ground cumin

2 cans (10½ ounces **each**) **Campbell's®** Condensed Beef Broth

2 large onions, sliced (about 2 cups)

1 can (about 15 ounces) whole peeled tomatoes

1 can (about 15 ounces) red kidney beans, rinsed and drained

¾ cup **uncooked** regular long-grain white rice

MAKES 8 SERVINGS

PREP TIME
15 MINUTES

COOK TIME
8 HOURS

1. Cut **4** evenly-spaced slits in the beef. Insert **1** garlic clove into **each** slit. Mix the chili powder, coriander and cumin in a small bowl. Rub the chili powder mixture over the beef. Place the beef into a 6-quart **CROCK-POT®** slow cooker.

2. Mix the broth, onions, tomatoes, beans and rice in a medium bowl. Pour over the beef.

3. Cover and cook on LOW for 8 to 9 hours* or until the beef is fork-tender.

Or on HIGH for 4 to 5 hours.

Recipe courtesy of
Campbell's Kitchen

Beef Bourguignonne

MAKES 6 SERVINGS

PREP TIME
10 MINUTES

COOK TIME
8 HOURS

1   can (10¾ ounces) **Campbell's®** Condensed Golden Mushroom Soup

1   cup Burgundy *or* other dry red wine

2   cloves garlic, minced

1   teaspoon dried thyme leaves, crushed

2   cups small button mushrooms (about 6 ounces)

2   cups fresh *or* thawed frozen baby carrots

1   cup frozen small whole onions, thawed

1½ pounds beef top round steak, 1½-inches thick, cut into 1-inch pieces

1. Stir the soup, wine, garlic, thyme, mushrooms, carrots, onions and beef in 3½-quart **CROCK-POT®** slow cooker.

2. Cover and cook on LOW for 8 to 9 hours* or until the beef is fork-tender.

Or on HIGH for 4 to 5 hours.

Recipe courtesy of
Campbell's Kitchen

Braised Short Ribs with Red Wine Tomato Sauce

- 4 pounds beef short ribs, cut into serving-sized pieces
- 2⅔ cups **Prego**® Fresh Mushroom Italian Sauce
- 1 cup dry red wine
- 1 bag fresh **or** frozen whole baby carrots
- 1 large onion, chopped (about 1 cup)
- Hot cooked rice

1. Season the ribs as desired.

2. Stir the Italian sauce, wine, carrots and onion in a 3½-quart **CROCK-POT**® slow cooker. Add the ribs and turn to coat.

3. Cover and cook on LOW for 7 to 8 hours* or until the ribs are fork-tender. Serve with the rice.

Or on HIGH for 4 to 5 hours.

MAKES 8 SERVINGS
PREP TIME
10 MINUTES
COOK TIME
7 HOURS

Recipe courtesy of
Campbell's Kitchen

Peppered Beef Tips

MAKES 2 TO 3 SERVINGS

COOK TIME
8 TO 10 HOURS (LOW)

1 pound beef round tip roast **or** round steak, cut into 1- to 1½-inch pieces

2 cloves garlic, minced

Black pepper

1 can (10½ ounces) **Campbell's®** Condensed French Onion Soup, undiluted

1 can (10¾ ounces) **Campbell's®** Condensed Cream of Mushroom Soup, undiluted

Hot cooked noodles **or** rice

1. Place beef in **CROCK-POT®** slow cooker. Season with garlic and pepper. Pour soups over beef.

2. Cover; cook on LOW 8 to 10 hours. Serve over noodles.

Recipe courtesy of
Crock-Pot® Slow Cooker Kitchens

Swiss Steak Delight

- 1   boneless beef round steak (about 1½ pounds), cut into 6 pieces
- ½   pound new potatoes, cut into quarters
- 1½ cups fresh **or** frozen whole baby carrots
- 1   medium onion, sliced (about ½ cup)
- 1   can (14.5 ounces) diced tomatoes with Italian herbs
- 1   can (10¼ ounces) **Campbell's**® Beef Gravy

1. Cook the beef in 2 batches in a 12-inch nonstick skillet over medium-high heat until well browned on both sides.

2. Place the potatoes, carrots, onion and beef into a 3½-quart **CROCK-POT**® slow cooker. Stir the tomatoes and gravy in a medium bowl. Pour the gravy mixture over the beef and vegetables.

3. Cover and cook on LOW for 8 to 9 hours* or until the beef is fork-tender.

Or on HIGH for 4 to 5 hours.

Recipe courtesy of
Campbell's Kitchen

Beef Taco Casserole

MAKES 8 SERVINGS

PREP TIME
10 MINUTES

COOK TIME
7 HOURS 5 MINUTES

2 pounds ground beef

1 can (10¾ ounces) **Campbell's®** Condensed Tomato Soup (Regular *or* **Healthy Request®**)

½ cup water

1 can (14.5 ounces) diced tomatoes with green chilies

8 corn tortillas (6-inch), cut into ½-inch strips

1 cup shredded Cheddar cheese (4 ounces)

3 green onions, chopped (about ⅓ cup)

Sour cream

1. Cook the beef in 2 batches in large skillet over medium-high heat, stirring to separate the meat. Pour off any fat.

2. Mix the beef, soup, water, tomatoes and tortillas in 3½- to 5-quart **CROCK-POT®** slow cooker.

3. Cover and cook on LOW for 7 to 8 hours*. Stir in the cheese. Cover and cook for 5 minutes. Sprinkle with green onions and serve with the sour cream.

Or on HIGH 4 to 5 hours.

Recipe courtesy of
Campbell's Kitchen

Carne Rellenos

1 can (4 ounces) whole green chilies, drained

4 ounces cream cheese, softened

1 flank steak, about 2 pounds

1½ cups **Pace®** Picante Sauce

1. Slit whole chilies open on one side with sharp knife; stuff with cream cheese.

2. Open steak flat on sheet of waxed paper; score steak and turn over. Lay stuffed chilies across unscored side of steak. Roll up and tie with kitchen string.

3. Place steak in **CROCK-POT®** slow cooker; pour in picante sauce. Cover; cook on LOW for 6 to 8 hours or on HIGH for 3 to 4 hours or until done.

4. Remove steak and cut into 6 pieces. Serve with sauce.

MAKES 6 SERVINGS
PREP TIME
20 TO 30 MINUTES
COOK TIME
6 TO 8 HOURS (LOW)
OR
3 TO 4 HOURS (HIGH)

beef main dishes

133

Recipe courtesy of
Crock-Pot® Slow Cooker Kitchens

Chili Pulled Beef Sandwiches

MAKES 8 SERVINGS

PREP TIME
5 MINUTES

COOK TIME
7 HOURS 10 MINUTES

2 pounds boneless beef chuck roasts

1 tablespoon barbecue seasoning

1 can (19 ounces) **Campbell's® Chunky**™ Grilled Steak-Steak Chili with Beans

1 large onion, thinly sliced (about 1 cup)

1 package (14 ounces) **Pepperidge Farm®** Classic Hot Dog Buns

½ cup shredded Colby Jack cheese

1. Sprinkle the beef with the barbecue seasoning.

2. Stir the chili and onion in a 5-quart **CROCK-POT®** slow cooker. Add the beef and turn to coat.

3. Cover and cook on LOW for 7 to 8 hours* or until the beef is fork-tender.

4. Remove the beef from the **CROCK-POT®** slow cooker to a cutting board and let stand for 10 minutes. Using 2 forks shred the beef. Return the beef to the **CROCK-POT®** slow cooker. Serve the beef mixture on the buns with the cheese.

Or on HIGH for 3 to 4 hours.

Recipe courtesy of
Campbell's Kitchen

THE ORIGINAL SLOW COOKER

Slow-Cooked Autumn Brisket

- 1 boneless beef brisket (about 3 pounds)
- 1 small head cabbage (about 1 pound), cut into 8 wedges
- 1 large sweet potato (about ¾ pound), peeled and cut into 1-inch pieces
- 1 large onion, cut into 8 wedges
- 1 medium Granny Smith apple, cored and cut into 8 wedges
- 2 cans (10¾ ounces *each*) **Campbell's**® Condensed Cream of Celery Soup (Regular *or* 98% Fat Free)
- 1 cup water
- 2 teaspoons caraway seed (optional)

1. Place the brisket in a 6-quart **CROCK-POT**® slow cooker. Top with the cabbage, sweet potato, onion and apple. Stir the soup, water and caraway seed, if desired, in a small bowl. Pour the soup mixture over the brisket and vegetable mixture.

2. Cover and cook on LOW for 8 to 9 hours* or until the brisket is fork-tender. Season as desired.

Or on HIGH for 4 to 5 hours.

MAKES 8 SERVINGS
PREP TIME
20 MINUTES
COOK TIME
8 HOURS

Recipe courtesy of
Campbell's Kitchen

Picadillo

MAKES 8 SERVINGS

PREP TIME
15 MINUTES

COOK TIME
7 HOURS

1½ pounds ground beef

2 large onions, diced (about 2 cups)

1¾ cups **Swanson**® Beef Stock

1 jar (8 ounces) **Pace**® Picante Sauce

1 tablespoon tomato paste

1 tablespoon chili powder

1 teaspoon ground cumin

½ cup raisins

½ cup toasted slivered almonds

Hot cooked rice

1. Cook the beef and onions in a 12-inch skillet over medium-high heat until the beef is well browned, stirring often to separate the meat. Pour off any fat.

2. Stir the beef mixture, stock, picante sauce, tomato paste, chili powder, cumin and raisins in a 6-quart **CROCK-POT**® slow cooker.

3. Cover and cook on LOW for 7 to 8 hours*. Top the beef mixture with the almonds. Serve with the rice.

Or on HIGH for 4 to 5 hours.

*Recipe courtesy of
Campbell's Kitchen*

Sweet 'n' Spicy Barbecued Brisket Sandwich

1 (5-pound) trimmed beef brisket
  Ground black pepper
1 tablespoon garlic powder
2 cups **Pace**® Picante Sauce
½ cup packed brown sugar
½ cup Worcestershire sauce
10 sandwich rolls **or** hamburger rolls, split
  Prepared coleslaw

1. Season the beef with the black pepper and garlic powder and place into a 13×9×2-inch shallow baking dish.

2. Stir the picante sauce, brown sugar and Worcestershire in a small bowl. Spread the picante sauce mixture over the beef. Cover and refrigerate at least 8 hours or overnight.

3. Place the beef into a 7-quart **CROCK-POT**® slow cooker. Cover and cook on LOW for 8 to 9 hours* or until the beef is fork-tender. Remove the beef from the **CROCK-POT**® slow cooker to a cutting board and let stand for 10 minutes.

4. Thinly slice the beef across the grain, or, using 2 forks, shred the beef. Return the beef to the **CROCK-POT**® slow cooker. Divide the beef and juices among the rolls. Top the beef with the coleslaw.

Or on HIGH for 4 to 5 hours.

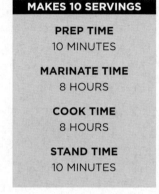

MAKES 10 SERVINGS

PREP TIME
10 MINUTES

MARINATE TIME
8 HOURS

COOK TIME
8 HOURS

STAND TIME
10 MINUTES

Recipe courtesy of
Campbell's Kitchen

Hot Beef Sandwiches au Jus

MAKES 8 TO 10 SERVINGS

PREP TIME
10 MINUTES

COOK TIME
6 TO 8 HOURS (HIGH)

4 pounds beef bottom round roast

2 cans (10½ ounces *each*) **Campbell's**® Condensed Beef Broth, undiluted

1 bottle (12 ounces) beer

2 envelopes (1 ounce *each*) dried onion-flavor soup mix

2 teaspoons sugar

1 teaspoon dried oregano

1 tablespoon minced garlic

Crusty French rolls, sliced in half

1. Trim excess fat from beef and discard. Place beef in **CROCK-POT**® slow cooker.

2. Combine broth, beer, soup mix, sugar, oregano and garlic in large mixing bowl. Pour mixture over beef. Cover; cook on HIGH 6 to 8 hours or until beef is fork-tender.

3. Remove beef from **CROCK-POT**® slow cooker; shred with 2 forks. Return beef to cooking liquid; mix well. Serve on crusty rolls with extra cooking liquid ("jus") on side for dipping.

Recipe courtesy of
Crock-Pot® Slow Cooker Kitchens

Melt-in-Your-Mouth Short Ribs

6   serving-sized pieces beef short ribs (about 3 pounds)

2   tablespoons packed brown sugar

3   cloves garlic, minced

1   teaspoon dried thyme leaves, crushed

¼   cup all-purpose flour

1   can (10½ ounces) **Campbell's®** Condensed French Onion Soup

1   bottle (12 fluid ounces) dark ale **or** beer

    Hot mashed potatoes **or** egg noodles

1. Place the beef into a 5-quart **CROCK-POT®** slow cooker. Add the brown sugar, garlic, thyme and flour and toss to coat.

2. Stir the soup and ale in a small bowl. Pour over the beef.

3. Cover and cook on LOW for 8 to 9 hours* or until the beef is fork-tender. Serve with the mashed potatoes.

Or on HIGH for 4 to 5 hours.

MAKES 6 SERVINGS
PREP TIME
10 MINUTES
COOK TIME
8 HOURS

beef main dishes

Recipe courtesy of
Campbell's Kitchen

pork main dishes

Fall-off-the-Bone BBQ Ribs

MAKES 6 TO 8 SERVINGS

PREP TIME
30 MINUTES

COOK TIME
3½ HOURS (HIGH)

½ cup paprika

⅜ cup sugar

¼ cup onion powder

1½ teaspoons salt

1½ teaspoons black pepper

2½ pounds pork baby back ribs, silver skin removed

2½ cups beer or **Swanson**® Beef Broth (Regular, 50% Less Sodium *or* Certified Organic)

1 quart barbecue sauce

½ cup honey

Sesame seeds *and* chopped chives (optional)

1. Preheat grill. Lightly oil grill grate.

2. Meanwhile, combine paprika, sugar, onion powder, salt and pepper in small bowl. Generously season ribs with dry rub mixture. Place ribs on grate. Cook for 3 minutes on each side or until ribs have grill marks.

3. Portion ribs into sections of **3** to **4** bones. Place in **CROCK-POT**® slow cooker. Pour beer or broth over ribs. Cover; cook on HIGH 2 hours. Combine barbecue sauce and honey in medium bowl and add to **CROCK-POT**® slow cooker. Cover; cook 1½ hours longer. Sprinkle with sesame seeds and chives, if desired. Serve with extra sauce on the side.

Recipe courtesy of
Crock-Pot® Slow Cooker Kitchens

Asian Pork Ribs with Spicy Noodles

MAKES 4 SERVINGS

PREP TIME
20 MINUTES

COOK TIME
8 TO 10 HOURS (LOW)
OR
5 TO 6 HOURS (HIGH)

2¾ ounces **Swanson**® Beef Broth (Regular, 50% Less Sodium **or** Certified Organic)

½ cup water

¼ cup rice wine vinegar

1 ounce (2-inch piece) fresh ginger, peeled and grated

1 cup (about 1 ounce) dried sliced shiitake mushrooms

¼ teaspoon red pepper flakes

1 tablespoon Chinese five-spice powder

1 teaspoon ground ginger

1 teaspoon chili powder

1 tablespoon dark sesame oil

2 full racks pork back ribs (about 4 pounds *total*)

¾ cup hoisin sauce, divided

1 pound (16 ounces) thin spaghetti, cooked according to package directions

¼ cup thinly sliced green onions

¼ cup chopped fresh cilantro

1. Stir together beef broth, water, rice wine vinegar, grated ginger, shiitake mushrooms and red pepper flakes in **CROCK-POT**® slow cooker.

2. Stir together five-spice powder, ground ginger, chili powder and sesame oil to form a paste. Blot ribs dry with paper towels. Rub both sides with spice paste and brush with half of hoisin sauce.

3. Place ribs in **CROCK-POT**® slow cooker with prepared cooking liquid (do not stir). Cover and cook on LOW 8 to 10 hours or on HIGH 5 to 6 hours or until meat is tender when pierced with a fork. Remove ribs to platter and brush lightly with remaining hoisin sauce. Keep warm until serving. Meanwhile, skim off any fat from cooking liquid.

4. Place warm spaghetti in shallow bowl. Ladle some hot broth over spaghetti and sprinkle with green onions and cilantro. Slice ribs and serve over pasta.

Recipe courtesy of
Crock-Pot® Slow Cooker Kitchens

Pork Chops with Jalapeño-Pecan Corn Bread Stuffing

MAKES 6 SERVINGS

COOK TIME
5 HOURS (LOW)

tip

For a more moist dressing, increase chicken broth to 1½ cups.

6 boneless pork loin chops, cut 1-inch thick (about 1½ pounds total)

¾ cup chopped onion

¾ cup chopped celery

½ cup coarsely chopped pecans

½ jalapeño pepper, seeded and chopped*

1 teaspoon rubbed sage

½ teaspoon dried rosemary

⅛ teaspoon black pepper

4 cups unseasoned corn bread stuffing mix

1¼ cups **Swanson® Natural Goodness®** Chicken Broth

1 egg, lightly beaten

*Jalapeño peppers can sting and irritate the skin, so wear rubber gloves when handling peppers and do not touch your eyes.

1. Trim excess fat from pork and discard. Coat large skillet with nonstick cooking spray; heat over medium heat. Add pork; cook 10 minutes or until browned on both sides. Transfer pork to plate.

2. Add onion, celery, pecans, jalapeño, sage, rosemary and black pepper to skillet. Cook 5 minutes or until onion and celery are tender.

3. Combine corn bread stuffing mix, vegetable mixture and broth in medium bowl. Stir in egg. Spoon stuffing mixture into **CROCK-POT®** slow cooker. Arrange pork on top. Cover; cook on LOW about 5 hours or until pork is tender.

Recipe courtesy of
Crock-Pot® Slow Cooker Kitchens

Pork Roast Landaise

MAKES 4 TO 6 SERVINGS

COOK TIME
8 HOURS (LOW) OR
4 HOURS (HIGH)

2 tablespoons olive oil

2½ pounds boneless center-cut pork loin roast

Salt *and* black pepper, to taste

1 medium onion, diced

2 large cloves garlic, minced

2 teaspoons dried thyme

2 parsnips, cut into ¾-inch slices

¼ cup red wine vinegar

¼ cup sugar

½ cup port *or* sherry wine

2 cups **Swanson**® Chicken Broth (Regular, **Natural Goodness**® *or* Certified Organic), divided

2 tablespoons cornstarch

3 pears, cored and sliced ¾ inch thick

1½ cups pitted prunes

1. Heat oil in large saucepan over medium-high heat. Season pork roast with salt and pepper; brown roast on all sides in saucepan. Place roast in **CROCK-POT**® slow cooker.

2. Add onion and garlic to saucepan. Cook and stir over medium heat 2 to 3 minutes. Stir in thyme. Transfer to **CROCK-POT**® slow cooker. Add parsnips; stir well.

3. Combine vinegar and sugar in same saucepan. Cook over medium heat, stirring constantly, until mixture thickens into syrup. Add port and cook 1 minute more. Add **1¾ cups** chicken broth. Combine remaining ¼ **cup** of broth with cornstarch in small bowl. Whisk in cornstarch mixture, and cook until smooth and slightly thickened. Pour into **CROCK-POT**® slow cooker.

4. Cover; cook on LOW 8 hours or on HIGH 4 hours. Add pears and prunes during last 30 minutes of cooking.

Recipe courtesy of
Crock-Pot® Slow Cooker Kitchens

Rigatoni with Broccoli Rabe and Sausage

MAKES 6 SERVINGS

COOK TIME

4 HOURS (LOW)
OR
2 HOURS (HIGH)

2 tablespoons olive oil

3 sweet **or** hot Italian sausage links, casings removed

2 cloves garlic, minced

1 large bunch (about 1¼ pounds) broccoli rabe

½ cup **Swanson**® Chicken Broth (Regular, **Natural Goodness**® **or** Certified Organic) **or** water

½ teaspoon salt

½ teaspoon red pepper flakes

1 pound **uncooked** rigatoni

Grated Parmesan cheese (optional)

1. Lightly coat interior of **CROCK-POT**® slow cooker with nonstick cooking spray. Set aside.

2. Heat oil in large skillet over medium heat. Add sausage and cook, stirring to break up sausage with spoon, until lightly browned, about 6 minutes. Add garlic and stir until softened and fragrant, about 1 minute. Transfer to lightly prepared **CROCK-POT**® slow cooker.

3. Trim any stiff, woody parts from bottoms of broccoli rabe stems and discard. Cut broccoli rabe into 1-inch lengths. Place in large bowl of cold water. Stir with hands to wash well. Lift broccoli rabe out of water by handfuls, leaving any sand or dirt in bottom of bowl. Shake well to remove excess water, but do not dry. Add to **CROCK-POT**® slow cooker with sausage. Pour in broth and sprinkle with salt and red pepper flakes. Cover; cook on LOW 4 hours or on HIGH 2 hours.

4. Meanwhile, cook rigatoni according to package directions. Stir into sausage mixture just before serving. Serve garnished, as desired, with Parmesan cheese.

Recipe courtesy of
Crock-Pot® Slow Cooker Kitchens

Rosemary Pork with Red Wine Risotto

MAKES 4 TO 6 SERVINGS

PREP TIME
15 MINUTES

COOK TIME
3 TO 4 HOURS (HIGH)

1 boneless pork loin (about 3 pounds)

1 teaspoon salt

1 teaspoon black pepper

2 tablespoons olive oil

6 sprigs fresh rosemary, divided

2 cups **Swanson**® Chicken Broth (Regular, **Natural Goodness**® *or* Certified Organic), divided

2 tablespoons butter, divided

3 cloves garlic, minced

½ cup minced onion

1 cup Arborio rice

1 cup fruity red wine

¾ cup grated Parmesan cheese

1. Season pork with salt and pepper. Heat oil in large skillet over medium-high heat until hot. Add 3 sprigs of rosemary and place pork roast on top. Brown pork roast on all sides, about 5 to 7 minutes. Transfer roast and rosemary to **CROCK-POT**® slow cooker.

2. Add ¼ **cup** broth to skillet. Cook and stir, loosening browned bits. Add **1 tablespoon** butter, garlic and onion. Cook and stir until onion is translucent.

3. Add rice to skillet. Cook and stir until rice just begins to brown, about 2 minutes. Stir in wine and remaining **1¾ cups** broth. Pour mixture around roast. Cover; cook on HIGH 3 to 4 hours, stirring occasionally, until roast reaches 160°F on thermometer inserted into center.

4. Remove and discard rosemary. Transfer roast to serving platter. Let stand 10 minutes before slicing.

5. Stir remaining **1 tablespoon** butter and Parmesan cheese into rice. Serve risotto with roast and garnish with remaining rosemary.

Recipe courtesy of
Crock-Pot**® **Slow Cooker Kitchens

CROCK·POT
· THE ORIGINAL SLOW COOKER ·

Campbell's

Shredded Pork Burritos with Green Chile Sauce

MAKES 12 SERVINGS

PREP TIME
20 MINUTES

COOK TIME
8 HOURS 15 MINUTES

STAND TIME
10 MINUTES

1 tablespoon vegetable oil

1 large onion, chopped (about 1 cup)

4 cloves garlic, minced

2 jars (16 ounces *each*) **Pace**® Picante Sauce

1 cup water

1 medium red pepper, chopped (about 1 cup)

8 green onions, chopped (about 1 cup)

1 bunch fresh cilantro leaves, chopped (about 1 cup)

¼ cup lemon pepper seasoning

¼ cup ground cumin

¼ cup chili powder

1 tablespoon lime juice

1 boneless pork loin roast (about 4 pounds), netted *or* tied

1 can (4 ounces) diced green chiles, drained

12 flour tortillas (10-inch), warmed

2 cups shredded Monterey Jack cheese (about 8 ounces)

1. Heat the oil in a 12-inch skillet over medium heat. Add the onion and garlic and cook until they're tender. Stir the picante sauce, water, red pepper, green onions, cilantro, lemon pepper, cumin, chili powder and lime juice in the skillet.

2. Place the pork into a 5-quart **CROCK-POT**® slow cooker. Pour the picante sauce mixture over the pork.

3. Cover and cook on LOW for 8 to 9 hours* or until the pork is fork-tender.

4. Remove the pork from the **CROCK-POT**® slow cooker to a cutting board and let stand for 10 minutes. Using 2 forks, shred the pork.

5. Spoon **5 cups** picante sauce mixture into a 2-quart saucepan. Stir in the chiles and cook over medium-high heat to a boil. Reduce the heat to low. Cook and stir for 15 minutes or until the mixture thickens.

6. Spoon **1 cup** pork down the center of **each** tortilla. Top **each** with **2 tablespoons** green chile sauce. Fold the sides of the tortillas over the filling and then fold up the ends to enclose the filling. Divide the remaining green chile sauce and the cheese over the burritos.

Or on HIGH for 4 to 5 hours.

Recipe courtesy of
Campbell's Kitchen

Slow-Cooked Pulled Pork Sliders

MAKES 12 MINI SANDWICHES

PREP TIME
10 MINUTES

COOK TIME
8 HOURS

STAND TIME
10 MINUTES

1 can (10¾ ounces) **Campbell's®** Condensed Tomato Soup

½ cup packed brown sugar

¼ cup cider vinegar

1 teaspoon garlic powder

1 boneless pork shoulder roast (3½ to 4½ pounds)

2 packages (15 ounces *each*) **Pepperidge Farm®** Slider Mini Sandwich Rolls

Hot pepper sauce (optional)

1. Stir the soup, brown sugar, vinegar and garlic powder in a 6-quart **CROCK-POT®** slow cooker. Add the pork and turn to coat.

2. Cover and cook on LOW for 8 to 9 hours* or until the pork is fork-tender. Spoon off any fat.

3. Remove the pork from the **CROCK-POT®** slow cooker to a cutting board and let stand for 10 minutes. Using 2 forks, shred the pork. Return the pork to the **CROCK-POT®** slow cooker.

4. Divide the pork mixture among the rolls. Serve with the hot pepper sauce, if desired.

Or on HIGH for 5 to 6 hours.

Recipe courtesy of
Campbell's Kitchen

Slow-Cooked Pulled Pork Sandwiches

MAKES 12 SERVINGS

PREP TIME
15 MINUTES

COOK TIME
8 HOURS

STAND TIME
10 MINUTES

1 tablespoon vegetable oil

1 boneless pork shoulder roast (3½ to 4 pounds), netted **or** tied

1 can (10½ ounces) **Campbell's**® Condensed French Onion Soup

1 cup ketchup

¼ cup cider vinegar

3 tablespoons packed brown sugar

12 round sandwich rolls **or** hamburger rolls, split

1. Heat the oil in a 10-inch skillet over medium-high heat. Add the pork and cook until it's well browned on all sides.

2. Stir the soup, ketchup, vinegar and brown sugar in a 5-quart **CROCK-POT**® slow cooker. Add the pork and turn to coat.

3. Cover and cook on LOW for 8 to 9 hours* or until the pork is fork-tender.

4. Remove the pork from the **CROCK-POT**® slow cooker to a cutting board and let stand for 10 minutes. Using 2 forks, shred the pork. Return the pork to the **CROCK-POT**® slow cooker.

5. Spoon the pork and sauce mixture on the rolls.

Or on HIGH for 4 to 5 hours.

Recipe courtesy of
Campbell's Kitchen

Apricot Glazed Pork Roast

MAKES 8 SERVINGS

PREP TIME
5 MINUTES

COOK TIME
8 HOURS

1 can (10½ ounces) **Campbell's®** Condensed Chicken Broth

1 jar (18 ounces) apricot preserves

1 large onion, chopped (about 1 cup)

2 tablespoons Dijon-style mustard

1 boneless pork loin roast (about 4 pounds)

1. Stir the broth, preserves, onion and mustard in a 3½-quart **CROCK-POT®** slow cooker. Add the pork to the **CROCK-POT®** slow cooker, cutting to fit, if needed, and turn to coat.

2. Cover and cook on LOW for 8 to 9 hours* or until the pork is fork-tender.

Or on HIGH for 4 to 5 hours.

tip

*For a thicker sauce, mix **2 tablespoons** cornstarch and **2 tablespoons** water in a small bowl until smooth. Remove the pork from the **CROCK-POT®** slow cooker. Stir the cornstarch mixture in the **CROCK-POT®** slow cooker. Cover and cook on HIGH for 10 minutes or until the mixture boils and thickens.*

Recipe courtesy of **Campbell's Kitchen**

Slow Cooker Pork Chops

- 6 bone-in pork chops (about 2 pounds)
- 1 medium onion, chopped (about ½ cup)
- 1 can (10¾ ounces) **Campbell's**® Condensed Cream of Mushroom Soup (Regular **or** 98% Fat Free)
- 1 can (10¾ ounces) **Campbell's**® Condensed Cream of Celery Soup (Regular **or** 98% Fat Free)

  Hot cooked instant white rice

1. Layer the pork and onion in a 3½-quart **CROCK-POT**® slow cooker. Stir the soups in a small bowl. Pour the soup mixture over all.

2. Cover and cook on LOW for 8 to 9 hours* or until the pork is fork-tender. Serve the pork and sauce with the rice.

Or on HIGH for 5 to 6 hours.

MAKES 6 SERVINGS

PREP TIME
5 MINUTES

COOK TIME
8 HOURS

Recipe courtesy of
Campbell's Kitchen

Big Al's Hot and Sweet Sausage Sandwich

MAKES 8 TO 10 SERVINGS

PREP TIME
15 MINUTES

COOK TIME
8 TO 10 HOURS (LOW)
OR
4 TO 6 HOURS (HIGH)

4 to 5 pounds hot Italian sausages

1 jar (26 ounces) **Prego**® Traditional Italian Sauce

1 large Vidalia onion (**or** other sweet onion), sliced

1 green bell pepper, cored, seeded and sliced

1 red bell pepper, cored, seeded and sliced

¼ cup packed dark brown sugar

Italian rolls, cut in half

Provolone cheese, sliced (optional)

1. Combine sausages, Italian sauce, onion, bell peppers and sugar in **CROCK-POT**® slow cooker. Cover; cook on LOW 8 to 10 hours or on HIGH 4 to 6 hours.

2. Place sausages on rolls. Top with vegetable mixture. Add provolone cheese, if desired.

Recipe courtesy of
Crock-Pot® Slow Cooker Kitchens

Mango Ginger Pork Roast

MAKES 4 TO 6 SERVINGS

PREP TIME
5 MINUTES

COOK TIME
6 TO 8 HOURS (LOW)
PLUS
3 TO 4 HOURS (HIGH)

1 pork shoulder roast (about 4 pounds)

½ to 1 teaspoon ground ginger, *or* to taste

Salt *and* black pepper, to taste

2 cups **Pace**® Pineapple Mango Chipotle Salsa

2 tablespoons honey

¼ cup apricot preserves

Hot cooked rice

1. Season roast with ginger, salt and pepper. Transfer to **CROCK-POT**® slow cooker.

2. Combine salsa, honey and preserves. Pour over roast. Cover; cook on LOW 6 to 8 hours. Turn **CROCK-POT**® slow cooker to HIGH and cook 3 to 4 hours longer, or until roast is tender. Serve with rice.

Recipe courtesy of
Crock-Pot® Slow Cooker Kitchens

Scalloped Potatoes and Ham

6 large russet potatoes, sliced into ¼-inch rounds

1 ham steak (about 1½ pounds), cut into cubes

1 can (10¾ ounces) **Campbell's**® Condensed Cream of Mushroom Soup (Regular **or** 98% Fat Free), undiluted

1 soup can water

1 cup (about 4 ounces) shredded Cheddar cheese

Grill seasoning, to taste

MAKES 5 TO 6 SERVINGS

COOK TIME
3½ HOURS (HIGH)
PLUS 1 HOUR (LOW)

1. Coat **CROCK-POT**® slow cooker with nonstick cooking spray. Arrange potatoes and ham in layers in **CROCK-POT**® slow cooker.

2. Combine soup, water, cheese and grill seasoning in medium bowl; pour over potatoes and ham. Cover; cook on HIGH about 3½ hours or until potatoes are fork-tender. Turn heat to LOW and cook 1 hour.

pork main dishes

163

Recipe courtesy of
Crock-Pot® **Slow Cooker Kitchens**

Hoppin' John

MAKES 6 SERVINGS

COOK TIME
3 TO 4 HOURS (LOW)

1 package (1 pound) andouille *or* smoked sausage, sliced

2½ cups **Swanson**® Chicken Broth (Regular, **Natural Goodness**® *or* Certified Organic), divided

2 cans (15 ounces *each*) black-eyed peas, rinsed and drained

1 box (about 8 ounces) dirty rice mix

½ cup salsa

½ to ¾ cup lump crabmeat (optional)

1. Cook sausage in large skillet over medium heat, stirring frequently, 5 minutes or until browned all over. Transfer to **CROCK-POT**® slow cooker with slotted spoon; discard any drippings from pan. Return skillet to heat and pour in ½ **cup** chicken broth. Cook and stir scraping up any browned bits from skillet. Pour over sausage.

2. Stir black-eyed peas, rice mix, remaining chicken broth and salsa into **CROCK-POT**® slow cooker with sausage. Cover and cook on LOW 3 to 4 hours or until rice is tender. Add crabmeat, if desired, and stir until well combined. Cover and cook until heated through, about 5 minutes.

Recipe courtesy of
Crock-Pot**® **Slow Cooker Kitchens

Backroads Ham and Potato Casserole

MAKES 4 TO 6 SERVINGS

PREP TIME
15 MINUTES

COOK TIME
3 TO 5 HOURS (HIGH)

2 pounds baking potatoes, cut into 1-inch cubes

½ teaspoon dried thyme

12 ounces cubed ham

1 can (10¾ ounces) **Campbell's**® Condensed Cream of Chicken Soup (Regular **or** 98% Fat Free), undiluted

4 ounces cream cheese, cut into ½-inch cubes

½ cup finely chopped green onions

½ cup frozen green peas, thawed

1. Coat **CROCK-POT**® slow cooker with nonstick cooking spray. Place potatoes in bottom. Add thyme and ham. Spread soup evenly over potatoes and ham. Cover; cook on HIGH 3 to 5 hours.

2. Gently stir in cream cheese, green onions and peas. Cover; cook 5 minutes longer or until cheese is melted.

Recipe courtesy of
Crock-Pot® Slow Cooker Kitchens

Golden Mushroom Pork & Apples

2 cans (10¾ ounces **each**) **Campbell's**® Condensed Golden Mushroom Soup

½ cup water

1 tablespoon packed brown sugar

1 tablespoon Worcestershire sauce

1 teaspoon dried thyme leaves, crushed

8 boneless pork chops, ¾-inch thick (about 2 pounds)

4 large Granny Smith apples, sliced

2 large onions, sliced (about 2 cups)

1. Stir the soup, water, brown sugar, Worcestershire and thyme in a 3½-quart **CROCK-POT**® slow cooker. Add the pork, apples and onions.

2. Cover and cook on LOW for 8 to 9 hours* or until the pork is cooked through.

*Or on HIGH for 4 to 5 hours.

Recipe courtesy of
Campbell's Kitchen

Savory Sausage with Onions and Peppers

MAKES 8 SERVINGS

PREP TIME
15 MINUTES

COOK TIME
7 HOURS

2 jars (1 pound 10 ounces *each*) **Prego**® Traditional Italian Sauce

3 large onions, sliced (about 3 cups)

3 large green *and/or* red peppers, cut into 2-inch-long strips (about 6 cups)

3 pounds sweet *or* hot Italian pork sausages, cut into 4-inch-long pieces

8 long hard rolls, split *or* hot cooked spaghetti

Grated Parmesan cheese

1. Stir the Italian sauce, onions, peppers and sausage in a 6-quart **CROCK-POT**® slow cooker.

2. Cover and cook on LOW for 7 to 8 hours* or until the sausage is cooked through. Spoon the sausage mixture into the rolls or serve it over the spaghetti. Top with the cheese.

Or on HIGH for 4 to 5 hours.

tip

For more overall flavor and color, brown the sausage before adding to the CROCK-POT® slow cooker.

Recipe courtesy of
Campbell's Kitchen

poultry
main dishes

Thai Chicken

MAKES 6 SERVINGS

PREP TIME
10 TO 15 MINUTES

COOK TIME
8 TO 9 HOURS (LOW)
OR
3 TO 4 HOURS (HIGH)

2½ pounds chicken pieces

1 cup **Pace**® Chunky Salsa

¼ cup peanut butter

2 tablespoons lime juice

1 tablespoon soy sauce

1 teaspoon minced fresh ginger

Hot cooked rice (optional)

½ cup peanuts, chopped

2 tablespoons chopped fresh cilantro

1. Place chicken in **CROCK-POT**® slow cooker. Mix together salsa, peanut butter, lime juice, soy sauce and ginger in small bowl; pour over chicken.

2. Cover; cook on LOW 8 to 9 hours or on HIGH 3 to 4 hours or until done.

3. Serve over rice, if desired, topped with sauce, peanuts and cilantro.

Recipe courtesy of
Crock-Pot® Slow Cooker
Kitchens

Chicken with Artichoke-Parmesan Dressing

MAKES 6 SERVINGS

PREP TIME
5 MINUTES

COOK TIME
3 HOURS (HIGH)

tip

Ground paprika helps to lend color, as well as flavor, to poultry, eliminating the need to brown the meat first.

2 cans (14 ounces *each*) quartered artichoke hearts, drained and coarsely chopped

4 ounces **Pepperidge Farm**® Herb Seasoned Stuffing

1½ cups frozen seasoning-blend vegetables, thawed*

¾ cup mayonnaise

¾ cup grated Parmesan cheese, divided

1 large egg, beaten

½ teaspoon paprika

½ teaspoon dried oregano

½ teaspoon salt

¼ teaspoon black pepper

6 bone-in chicken breast halves, rinsed and patted dry (about 3½ pounds)

Seasoning-blend vegetables are a mixture of chopped bell peppers, onions and celery. If you're unable to find frozen vegetables, use ½ cup each of fresh vegetables.

1. Coat **CROCK-POT**® slow cooker with cooking spray. Combine artichokes, stuffing, vegetables, mayonnaise, all but **1 tablespoon** Parmesan and egg in large bowl. Stir gently and blend well. Transfer mixture to **CROCK-POT**® slow cooker.

2. Combine paprika, oregano, salt and pepper in small bowl. Rub evenly onto chicken. Arrange chicken on artichoke mixture in **CROCK-POT**® slow cooker, overlapping slightly. Cover; cook on HIGH 3 hours.

3. Transfer chicken to serving platter. Cover with foil to keep warm. Stir artichoke mixture in **CROCK-POT**® slow cooker. Sprinkle evenly with remaining **1 tablespoon** Parmesan. Cook, uncovered, 20 to 25 minutes or until thickened. Serve dressing with chicken.

Recipe courtesy of
Crock-Pot® Slow Cooker Kitchens

Ham and Sage Stuffed Cornish Hens

MAKES 4 SERVINGS

PREP TIME
45 MINUTES

COOK TIME
5 TO 6 HOURS (LOW)
OR
3 TO 4 HOURS (HIGH)

1 cup *plus* 3 tablespoons sliced celery, divided

1 cup sliced leek (white part only)

2 tablespoons butter, divided

¼ cup finely diced onion

¼ cup diced smoked ham *or* prosciutto

1 cup seasoned stuffing mix

1 cup **Swanson**® Chicken Broth (Regular, **Natural Goodness**® *or* Certified Organic)

1 tablespoon finely chopped fresh sage leaves *or* 1 teaspoon ground sage

4 Cornish hens (about 1½ pounds *each*)

Salt

Black pepper

1. Coat **CROCK-POT**® slow cooker with nonstick cooking spray. Toss **1 cup** celery and **1 cup** leek in **CROCK-POT**® slow cooker.

2. Melt **1 tablespoon** butter in large nonstick skillet over medium heat. Add remaining **3 tablespoons** celery, onion and ham. Cook, stirring frequently, 5 minutes or until onion is soft. Stir in stuffing mix, chicken broth and sage. Transfer mixture to medium bowl.

3. Rinse hens and pat dry; sprinkle inside and out with salt and pepper. Gently spoon stuffing into birds' cavities. Tie each hen's drumsticks together with kitchen twine.

4. Melt remaining **1 tablespoon** butter in same skillet over medium-high heat. Place **2** hens, breast sides down, in skillet and cook until skins brown, turning to brown all sides. Transfer to prepared **CROCK-POT**® slow cooker. Repeat with remaining hens. Cover and cook on LOW 5 to 6 hours on HIGH 3 to 4 hours. Remove twine and place hens on serving platter with vegetables; spoon cooking broth over hens.

Recipe courtesy of
Crock-Pot® Slow Cooker
Kitchens

Slow Cooker Cheesy Chicken & Tortillas

MAKES 6 SERVINGS

PREP TIME
10 MINUTES

COOK TIME
4 HOURS 30 MINUTES

4 skinless, boneless chicken breast halves (about 1 pound)

1 package (about 1 ounce) mild taco seasoning mix

5¼ cups **Swanson**® Chicken Stock

2 tablespoons butter

2 cans (10¾ ounces *each*) **Campbell's**® Condensed Cream of Chicken Soup (Regular *or* 98% Fat Free)

10 fajita-size flour tortillas (10-inch), cut into 1-inch pieces

4 cups shredded Mexican cheese blend (about 16 ounces)

Hot cooked regular long-grain white rice

1. Place the chicken into a 3½-quart **CROCK-POT**® slow cooker. Top with all but **2 tablespoons** of the taco seasoning. Pour **3½ cups** of the stock over the chicken.

2. Cover and cook on LOW for 4 to 5 hours or until the chicken is cooked through. Remove the chicken to a cutting board. Using 2 forks, shred the chicken.

Recipe courtesy of
Campbell's Kitchen

3. Heat the oven to 350°F.

4. Heat the butter in a 3-quart saucepan over medium heat. Stir the remaining taco seasoning, stock and soup in the saucepan. Stir in the chicken.

5. Layer **half** of the chicken mixture, tortillas and cheese in a 3-quart shallow baking dish. Repeat the layers. Bake for 30 minutes or until the mixture is hot and bubbling. Serve over the rice.

CROCK·POT®
· THE ORIGINAL SLOW COOKER ·

Campbell's

Chicken Sausage Pilaf

1 pound **uncooked** chicken **or** turkey sausage, casings removed

1 package (about 7 ounces) **uncooked** chicken-flavored rice and vermicelli pasta mix

4 cups **Swanson**® Chicken Broth (Regular, **Natural Goodness**® **or** Certified Organic)

2 stalks celery, diced

¼ cup slivered almonds

Salt **and** black pepper

MAKES 4 SERVINGS

COOK TIME
7 TO 10 HOURS (LOW)
OR
3 TO 4 HOURS (HIGH)

1. Brown sausage in large skillet over medium-high heat, stirring to break up meat. Drain fat. Add rice and pasta mix to skillet. Cook and stir 1 minute.

2. Place mixture in **CROCK-POT**® slow cooker. Add broth, celery, almonds, salt and pepper to **CROCK-POT**® slow cooker; mix well.

3. Cover; cook on LOW 7 to 10 hours or on HIGH 3 to 4 hours or until rice is tender.

Recipe courtesy of
Crock-Pot*® *Slow Cooker Kitchens

Pacific Island Chicken & Rice

poultry main dishes

178

MAKES 8 SERVINGS

PREP TIME
20 MINUTES

COOK TIME
7 HOURS

2 cans (10½ ounces *each*) **Campbell's**® Condensed Chicken Broth

1 cup water

¼ cup soy sauce

2 cloves garlic, minced

8 skinless, boneless chicken thighs (about 2 pounds), cut into 1½-inch pieces

1 medium green *or* red pepper, cut into 1½-inch pieces (about 1 cup)

4 green onions, cut into 2-inch pieces (about 1 cup)

1 can (20 ounces) pineapple chunks in juice, undrained

1 cup *uncooked* regular long-grain white rice

Toasted sliced almonds

1. Stir the broth, water, soy sauce, garlic, chicken, pepper, onions, pineapple with juice and rice in 6-quart **CROCK-POT**® slow cooker.

2. Cover and cook on LOW for 7 to 8 hours* or until chicken is cooked through.

3. Sprinkle with the almonds before serving.

Or on HIGH for 4 to 5 hours.

tip

To toast almonds, arrange almonds in single layer in a shallow baking pan. Bake at 350°F. for 10 minutes or until lightly browned.

Recipe courtesy of
Campbell's Kitchen

Chicken in Creamy Sun-Dried Tomato Sauce

MAKES 8 SERVINGS

PREP TIME
15 MINUTES

COOK TIME
7 HOURS

2 cans (10¾ ounces *each*) **Campbell's**® Condensed Cream of Chicken with Herbs Soup *or* **Campbell's**® Condensed Cream of Chicken Soup

1 cup Chablis *or* other dry white wine*

¼ cup coarsely chopped pitted kalamata *or* oil-cured olives

2 tablespoons drained capers

2 cloves garlic, minced

1 can (14 ounces) artichoke hearts, drained and chopped

1 cup drained and coarsely chopped sun-dried tomatoes

8 skinless, boneless chicken breast halves (about 2 pounds)

½ cup chopped fresh basil leaves (optional)

Hot cooked rice, egg noodles *or* mashed potatoes

*You can substitute **Swanson**® Chicken Broth for the wine, if desired.*

1. Stir the soup, wine, olives, capers, garlic, artichokes and tomatoes in a 3½-quart **CROCK-POT**® slow cooker. Add the chicken and turn to coat.

2. Cover and cook on LOW for 7 to 8 hours** or until the chicken is cooked through. Sprinkle with the basil, if desired. Serve with the rice.

**Or on HIGH for 4 to 5 hours.

Recipe courtesy of
Campbell's Kitchen

Golden Chicken with Noodles

2 cans (10¾ ounces **each**) **Campbell's®** Condensed Cream of Chicken Soup (Regular **or** 98% Fat Free)

½ cup water

¼ cup lemon juice

1 tablespoon Dijon-style mustard

1½ teaspoons garlic powder

8 large carrots, thickly sliced (about 6 cups)

8 skinless, boneless chicken breast halves (about 2 pounds)

4 cups egg noodles, cooked and drained

Chopped fresh parsley

1. Stir the soup, water, lemon juice, mustard, garlic powder and carrots in a 3½-quart **CROCK-POT®** slow cooker. Add the chicken and turn to coat.

2. Cover and cook on LOW for 7 to 8 hours* or until the chicken is cooked through. Serve with the noodles. Sprinkle with the parsley.

*Or on HIGH for 4 to 5 hours.

Recipe courtesy of
Campbell's Kitchen

Jambalaya

MAKES 6 SERVINGS

PREP TIME
25 MINUTES

COOK TIME
7 HOURS 10 MINUTES

3 cups **Swanson®** Chicken Stock

1 tablespoon Creole seasoning

1 large green pepper, diced (about 1½ cups)

1 large onion, diced (about 1 cup)

2 cloves garlic, minced

½ teaspoon ground black pepper

2 large stalks celery, diced (about 1 cup)

1 can (14.5 ounces) diced tomatoes

1 pound kielbasa, diced (about 3 cups)

6 skinless, boneless chicken thighs (about ¾ pound), cut into cubes

2 cups **uncooked** instant white rice

½ pound fresh medium shrimp, shelled and deveined

1. Stir the stock, Creole seasoning, green pepper, onion, garlic, black pepper, celery, tomatoes, kielbasa and chicken in a 5-quart **CROCK-POT®** slow cooker.

2. Cover and cook on LOW for 7 to 8 hours* or until the chicken is cooked through.

3. Stir the rice and shrimp in the cooker. Cover and cook for 10 minutes or until the shrimp are cooked through and the rice is tender.

Or on HIGH for 4 to 5 hours.

Recipe courtesy of
Campbell's Kitchen

Chicken & Bean Burritos

MAKES 12 SERVINGS

PREP TIME
10 MINUTES

COOK TIME
6 HOURS

1 can (10¾ ounces) **Campbell's**® Condensed Cheddar Cheese Soup

1 teaspoon garlic powder

2 tablespoons chili powder

2 pounds skinless, boneless chicken thighs, cut into 1-inch pieces

1 can (about 14 ounces) black beans, rinsed and drained

1 can (about 14 ounces) pinto beans, rinsed and drained

12 flour tortilla (8- to 10-inch), warmed

Chopped lettuce

Chopped tomato

1. Stir the soup, garlic powder, chili powder and chicken in a 3½- to 4-quart **CROCK-POT**® slow cooker.

2. Cover and cook on LOW for 6 to 7 hours* or until the chicken is cooked through.

3. Mash the black and pinto beans with a fork in a medium bowl. Stir into the chicken mixture. Spoon **about ½ cup** of the chicken mixture down the center of **each** tortilla. Top with the lettuce and tomato. Fold the tortillas around the filling.

Or on HIGH for 3 to 4 hours.

Recipe courtesy of
Campbell's Kitchen

Slow Cooker Orange Chicken

MAKES 4 SERVINGS

PREP TIME
10 MINUTES

COOK TIME
8 HOURS

1½ cups **Swanson®** Chicken Stock

¼ cup teriyaki sauce

3 cloves garlic, minced

¾ cup orange marmalade

4 green onions, sliced (about ½ cup)

2 tablespoons cornstarch

8 chicken thighs, skin removed (about 2 pounds)

½ cup walnut pieces

Hot cooked rice

1. Stir the stock, teriyaki sauce, garlic, marmalade, ¼ **cup** green onions and cornstarch in a 6-quart **CROCK-POT®** slow cooker. Add the chicken and turn to coat.

2. Cover and cook on LOW for 8 to 9 hours* or until the chicken is cooked through. Sprinkle with the walnuts and remaining green onions. Serve with the rice.

Or on HIGH for 4 to 5 hours.

Recipe courtesy of
Campbell's Kitchen

Slow Cooker Chicken Cacciatore

1½ cups **Swanson®** Chicken Stock

2 teaspoons garlic powder

2 cans (about 14.5 ounces *each*) diced Italian-style tomatoes

4 cups mushrooms, cut in half (about 12 ounces)

2 large onions, chopped (about 2 cups)

3 pounds chicken parts, skin removed

¼ cup cornstarch

1 package (16 ounces) spaghetti, cooked and drained

1. Stir **1 cup** stock, garlic powder, tomatoes, mushrooms and onions in a 5- to 6-quart **CROCK-POT®** slow cooker. Add the chicken and turn to coat.

2. Cover and cook on LOW for 7 to 8 hours* or until the chicken is cooked through. Remove the chicken from the **CROCK-POT®** slow cooker and keep warm.

3. Stir the cornstarch and remaining stock in a small bowl until the mixture is smooth. Stir the cornstarch mixture in the **CROCK-POT®** slow cooker. Cover and cook on HIGH for 10 minutes or until the mixture boils and thickens. Serve with the chicken and spaghetti.

Or on HIGH for 4 to 5 hours.

Recipe courtesy of
Campbell's Kitchen

Curried Turkey Cutlets

2 cans (10¾ ounces *each*) **Campbell's**® Condensed Cream of Chicken Soup (Regular *or* 98% Fat Free)

2 tablespoons water

1 tablespoon curry powder

½ teaspoon cracked black pepper

8 turkey breast cutlets (about 2 pounds)

¼ cup heavy cream

½ cup seedless red grapes, cut in half

Hot cooked rice *or* seasoned rice blend

1. Stir the soup, water, curry powder and black pepper in a 3½- to 4-quart **CROCK-POT**® slow cooker. Add the turkey and turn to coat.

2. Cover and cook on LOW for 6 to 7 hours* or until the turkey is cooked through.

3. Stir the cream and grapes into the **CROCK-POT**® cooker. Serve with the rice.

Or on HIGH for 3 to 4 hours.

MAKES 8 SERVINGS
PREP TIME
10 MINUTES
COOK TIME
6 HOURS

tip

*This recipe is delicious served with any of these toppers: chutney, toasted coconut, sliced almonds **and/or** raisins.*

Recipe courtesy of
Campbell's Kitchen

Slow Cooker Coq au Vin

MAKES 6 SERVINGS

PREP TIME
10 MINUTES

COOK TIME
8 HOURS

1 package (10 ounces) sliced mushrooms (about 3¾ cups)

1 bag (16 ounces) frozen whole small white onions

1 sprig fresh rosemary leaves

2 pounds skinless, boneless chicken breast halves **and/or** thighs, cut into 1-inch strips

¼ cup cornstarch

1 can (10¾ ounces) **Campbell's**® Condensed Golden Mushroom Soup

1 cup Burgundy **or** other dry red wine

Hot mashed **or** oven-roasted potatoes

1. Place the mushrooms, onions, rosemary and chicken into a 3½-quart **CROCK-POT**® slow cooker.

2. Stir the cornstarch, soup and wine in a small bowl. Pour over the chicken and vegetables.

3. Cover and cook on LOW for 8 to 9 hours*. Remove and discard the rosemary. Serve the chicken mixture with the mashed potatoes.

Or on HIGH for 4 to 5 hours.

Recipe courtesy of
Campbell's Kitchen

Herbed Turkey Breast

MAKES 8 SERVINGS

PREP TIME
10 MINUTES

COOK TIME
8 HOURS

STAND TIME
10 MINUTES

1 can (10¾ ounces) **Campbell's**® Condensed Cream of Mushroom Soup (Regular **or** 98% Fat Free)

½ cup water

4½- to 5-pound turkey breast

1 teaspoon poultry seasoning

1 tablespoon chopped fresh parsley

Hot mashed potatoes

1. Stir the soup and water in a 3½- to 6-quart **CROCK-POT**® slow cooker. Rinse the turkey with cold water and pat it dry. Rub the turkey with the poultry seasoning and place it into the **CROCK-POT**® slow cooker. Sprinkle with the parsley.

2. Cover and cook on LOW for 8 to 9 hours* or until the turkey is cooked through. Let the turkey stand for 10 minutes before slicing. Serve with the soup mixture and mashed potatoes.

Or on HIGH for 4 to 5 hours.

tip

If using a frozen turkey breast, thaw it before cooking.

Recipe courtesy of
Campbell's Kitchen

Turkey Fajita Wraps

MAKES 8 SERVINGS

PREP TIME
10 MINUTES

COOK TIME
6 HOURS

tip

Delicious served with an assortment of additional toppers: sliced green onions, sliced ripe olives, shredded lettuce, sliced jalapeño peppers, sour cream and/or chopped fresh cilantro.

2 cups **Pace**® Picante Sauce

2 large green *or* red peppers, cut into 2-inch-long strips (about 4 cups)

1½ cups frozen whole kernel corn, thawed

1 tablespoon chili powder

2 tablespoons lime juice

3 cloves garlic, minced

2 pounds turkey breast cutlets, cut into 4-inch-long strips

16 flour tortillas (8-inch), warmed

Shredded Mexican cheese blend

1. Stir the picante sauce, peppers, corn, chili powder, lime juice, garlic and turkey in a 4-quart **CROCK-POT**® slow cooker.

2. Cover and cook on LOW for 6 to 7 hours* or until the turkey is cooked through.

3. Spoon **about ½ cup** of the turkey mixture down the center of **each** tortilla. Top with the cheese. Fold the tortillas around the filling.

Or on HIGH for 3 to 4 hours.

Recipe courtesy of
Campbell's Kitchen

Nice 'n' Easy Italian Chicken

MAKES 4 SERVINGS

PREP TIME
10 MINUTES

COOK TIME
6 TO 8 HOURS (LOW)

4 boneless, skinless chicken breasts (about 1 pound)

8 ounces mushrooms, sliced

1 medium green bell pepper, chopped

1 medium zucchini, diced

1 medium onion, chopped

1 jar (26 ounces) **Prego**® Traditional Italian Sauce

Hot cooked linguini or spaghetti

Combine all ingredients except pasta in **CROCK-POT**® slow cooker. Cover; cook on LOW 6 to 8 hours or until chicken is tender. Serve over linguini.

Recipe courtesy of
Crock-Pot® Slow Cooker Kitchens

Slow Cooker Chicken and Dressing

4 boneless, skinless chicken breasts

Salt **and** black pepper

4 slices Swiss cheese

1 can (about 14 ounces) **Swanson**® Chicken Broth (Regular, **Natural Goodness**® **or** Certified Organic)

2 cans (10¾ ounces each) **Campbell's**® Condensed Cream of Chicken, Celery **or** Mushroom Soup (Regular **or** 98% Fat Free), undiluted

3 cups packaged stuffing mix

½ cup (1 stick) butter, melted

1. Place chicken in **CROCK-POT**® slow cooker. Season with salt and pepper.

2. Top **each** breast with cheese slice. Add broth and soup. Sprinkle stuffing mix over top; pour melted butter over all. Cover; cook on LOW 6 to 8 hours or on HIGH 3 to 4 hours.

MAKES 4 SERVINGS

PREP TIME
10 MINUTES

COOK TIME
6 TO 8 HOURS (LOW)
OR
3 TO 4 HOURS (HIGH)

poultry main dishes

197

Recipe courtesy of
Crock-Pot® Slow Cooker Kitchens

Turkey Breast with Barley-Cranberry Stuffing

MAKES 6 SERVINGS

COOK TIME
4 TO 6 HOURS (LOW)

tip

Browning poultry before cooking it in the CROCK-POT® slow cooker isn't necessary but helps to enhance the flavor and adds an oven-roasted appearance to the finished dish.

1 fresh **or** thawed frozen bone-in turkey breast half (about 2 pounds), skinned

2 cups **Swanson® Natural Goodness®** Chicken Broth

1 cup **uncooked** quick-cooking barley

½ cup chopped onion

½ cup dried cranberries

2 tablespoons slivered almonds, toasted*

½ teaspoon rubbed sage

½ teaspoon garlic-pepper seasoning

⅓ cup finely chopped fresh parsley

To toast almonds, spread in single layer on baking sheet. Bake in preheated 350°F oven 8 to 10 minutes or until golden brown, stirring frequently.

1. Thaw turkey breast, if frozen. Remove skin and discard.

2. Combine broth, barley, onion, cranberries, almonds, sage and garlic-pepper seasoning in **CROCK-POT®** slow cooker.

3. Coat large nonstick skillet with cooking spray. Heat over medium heat until hot. Brown turkey breast on all sides; add to **CROCK-POT®** slow cooker. Cover; cook on LOW 4 to 6 hours.

4. Transfer turkey to cutting board; cover with foil to keep warm. Let stand 10 to 15 minutes before carving. Stir parsley into cooking liquid in **CROCK-POT®** slow cooker. Serve over turkey and stuffing, if desired.

Recipe courtesy of
Crock-Pot® Slow Cooker Kitchens

Slow Cooker Chicken & Dumplings

MAKES 8 SERVINGS

PREP TIME
20 MINUTES

COOK TIME
7 HOURS 30 MINUTES

6 skinless, boneless chicken breast halves (about 1½ pounds), cut into 1-inch pieces

2 medium Yukon Gold potatoes, cut into 1-inch pieces (about 2 cups)

2 cups whole baby carrots

2 stalks celery, sliced (about 1 cup)

2 cans (10¾ ounces *each*) **Campbell's**® Condensed Cream of Chicken Soup (Regular *or* 98% Fat Free)

1 cup water

1 teaspoon dried thyme leaves, crushed

¼ teaspoon ground black pepper

2 cups all-purpose baking mix

⅔ cup milk

1. Place the chicken, potatoes, carrots and celery into a 6-quart **CROCK-POT**® slow cooker.

2. Stir the soup, water, thyme and black pepper in a small bowl. Pour the soup mixture over the chicken and vegetables.

3. Cover and cook on LOW for 7 to 8 hours* or until the chicken is cooked through.

4. Stir the baking mix and milk in a medium bowl. Drop the batter by spoonfuls onto the chicken mixture. Increase the heat to HIGH. Tilt the lid to vent and cook for 30 minutes or until the dumplings are cooked in the center.

Or on HIGH for 4 to 5 hours.

Recipe courtesy of
Campbell's Kitchen

CROCK·POT
THE ORIGINAL SLOW COOKER

Campbell's

Spicy Shredded Chicken

6 boneless, skinless chicken breasts (about 1½ pounds)

1 jar (16 ounces) **Pace®** Salsa

Flour tortillas, warmed

Optional toppings: shredded cheese, sour cream, shredded lettuce, diced tomato, diced onion **or** sliced avocado

1. Place chicken in **CROCK-POT®** slow cooker. Cover with salsa. Cover; cook on LOW 6 to 8 hours or until chicken is tender and no longer pink in center.

2. Shred chicken with 2 forks. Serve with warmed tortillas and top as desired.

Recipe courtesy of
Crock-Pot® Slow Cooker Kitchens

Easy Parmesan Chicken

MAKES 4 SERVINGS

PREP TIME
20 MINUTES

COOK TIME
6 TO 7 HOURS (LOW)
OR
3 TO 4 HOURS (HIGH)

tip

Dairy products should be added at the end of the cooking time because they will curdle if cooked in the CROCK-POT® slow cooker for a long time.

8 ounces mushrooms, sliced

1 medium onion, cut into thin wedges

1 tablespoon olive oil

4 boneless, skinless chicken breasts

1 jar (26 ounces) **Prego®** Traditional Italian Sauce

½ teaspoon dried basil

¼ teaspoon dried oregano

1 bay leaf

½ cup (2 ounces) shredded part-skim mozzarella cheese

¼ cup grated Parmesan cheese

Hot cooked spaghetti

1. Place mushrooms and onion in **CROCK-POT®** slow cooker.

2. Heat oil in large skillet over medium-high heat. Lightly brown chicken on both sides. Place chicken in **CROCK-POT®** slow cooker. Pour Italian sauce over chicken; add basil, oregano and bay leaf. Cover; cook on LOW 6 to 7 hours or on HIGH 3 to 4 hours, or until chicken is tender. Remove and discard bay leaf.

3. Sprinkle chicken with cheeses. Cook, uncovered, until cheeses melt. Serve over spaghetti.

Recipe courtesy of
Crock-Pot® Slow Cooker Kitchens

side dishes

Asian Golden Barley with Cashews

MAKES 4 SERVINGS

PREP TIME
20 MINUTES

COOK TIME
4 TO 5 HOURS (LOW)
OR
2 TO 3 HOURS (HIGH)

2 tablespoons unsalted butter

1 cup hulled barley, sorted

3 cups **Swanson**® Vegetable Broth (Regular *or* Certified Organic)

1 cup chopped celery

1 green bell pepper, cored, seeded and chopped

1 yellow onion, peeled and minced

1 clove garlic, minced

¼ teaspoon black pepper

¼ cup finely chopped cashews

1. Heat skillet over medium heat until hot. Add butter and barley. Cook and stir about 10 minutes or until barley is slightly browned. Transfer to **CROCK-POT**® slow cooker.

2. Add broth, celery, bell pepper, onion, garlic and black pepper. Stir well to combine. Cover; cook on LOW 4 to 5 hours or on HIGH 2 to 3 hours, or until barley is tender and liquid is absorbed.

3. To serve, garnish with cashews.

Recipe courtesy of
Crock-Pot® Slow Cooker Kitchens

Lemon Dilled Parsnips and Turnips

MAKES 8 TO 10 SERVINGS

PREP TIME
15 MINUTES

COOK TIME
3 TO 4 HOURS (LOW)
OR
1 TO 3 HOURS (HIGH)

2 cups **Swanson**® Chicken Broth (Regular, **Natural Goodness**® *or* Certified Organic)

¼ cup chopped green onions

4 tablespoons lemon juice

4 tablespoons dried dill

1 teaspoon minced garlic

4 turnips, peeled and cut into ½-inch pieces

3 parsnips, peeled and cut into ½-inch pieces

4 tablespoons cornstarch

¼ cup cold water

1. Combine broth, onions, lemon juice, dill and garlic in **CROCK-POT**® slow cooker.

2. Add turnips and parsnips; stir. Cover; cook on LOW 3 to 4 hours or on HIGH 1 to 3 hours.

3. Turn **CROCK-POT**® slow cooker to HIGH. Dissolve cornstarch in water. Add to **CROCK-POT**® slow cooker. Stir well to combine. Cover; continue cooking 15 minutes longer or until thickened.

Recipe courtesy of
Crock-Pot® Slow Cooker Kitchens

Artichoke and Tomato Paella

MAKES 8 SERVINGS

COOK TIME
4 HOURS (LOW) OR
2 HOURS (HIGH)

4 cups **Swanson**® Vegetable Broth (Regular *or* Certified Organic)

2 cups converted white rice

5 ounces (½ of a 10-ounce package) frozen chopped spinach, thawed and drained

1 green bell pepper, cored, seeded and chopped

1 medium ripe tomato, sliced into wedges

1 medium yellow onion, chopped

1 medium carrot, peeled and diced

3 cloves garlic, minced

1 tablespoon minced flat-leaf parsley

1 teaspoon salt

½ teaspoon black pepper

1 can (13¾ ounces) artichoke hearts, quartered, rinsed and well-drained

½ cup frozen peas

1. Combine broth, rice, spinach, bell pepper, tomato, onion, carrot, garlic, parsley, salt and pepper in **CROCK-POT**® slow cooker. Mix thoroughly. Cover; cook on LOW 4 hours or on HIGH 2 hours.

2. Before serving, add artichoke hearts and peas. Cover; cook on HIGH 15 minutes. Mix well before serving.

Recipe courtesy of
Crock-Pot® Slow Cooker Kitchens

Asparagus and Cheese

2 cups crushed saltine crackers

1 can (10¾ ounces) **Campbell's®** Condensed Cream of Asparagus Soup, undiluted

1 can (10¾ ounces) **Campbell's®** Condensed Cream of Chicken Soup (Regular *or* 98% Fat Free), undiluted

⅔ cup slivered almonds

4 ounces American cheese, cut into cubes

1 egg

1½ pounds fresh asparagus, trimmed

Combine crackers, soups, almonds, cheese and egg in large bowl; stir well. Pour into **CROCK-POT®** slow cooker. Add asparagus, and stir to coat. Cover; cook on HIGH 3 to 3½ hours or until asparagus is tender. Garnish as desired.

side dishes

210

tip

Cooking times are guidelines. ***CROCK-POT®*** *slow cookers, just like ovens, cook differently depending on a variety of factors. For example, cooking times will be longer at higher altitudes. You may need to slightly adjust cooking times for your* ***CROCK-POT®*** *slow cooker.*

Recipe courtesy of ***Crock-Pot® Slow Cooker Kitchens***

Manchego Eggplant

4 large eggplants

1 cup all-purpose flour

2 tablespoons olive oil

2 jars (25½ ounces *each*) **Prego**® Roasted Garlic and Herb Italian Sauce, divided

2 tablespoons Italian seasoning, divided

1 cup (4 ounces) grated manchego cheese, divided

MAKES 8 TO 10 SERVINGS

COOK TIME
2 HOURS (HIGH)

1. Peel eggplants and slice horizontally into ¾-inch-thick pieces. Place flour in shallow bowl. Dredge **each** slice of eggplant in flour to coat.

2. Heat oil in large skillet over medium-high heat. In batches, lightly brown eggplant on both sides.

3. Pour thin layer of Italian sauce into bottom of **CROCK-POT**® slow cooker. Top with eggplant slices, Italian seasoning, cheese and another layer of Italian sauce. Repeat layers until all ingredients have been used.

4. Cover and cook on HIGH 2 hours.

Recipe courtesy of
Crock-Pot® Slow Cooker Kitchens

side dishes

211

Polenta-Style Corn Casserole

side dishes

212

MAKES 6 SERVINGS

PREP TIME
15 MINUTES

COOK TIME
4 TO 5 HOURS (LOW)
OR
2 TO 3 HOURS (HIGH)

1 can (14½ ounces) **Swanson®** Chicken Broth (Regular, **Natural Goodness®** *or* Certified Organic)

½ cup cornmeal

1 can (7 ounces) corn, drained

1 can (4 ounces) diced green chiles, drained

¼ cup diced red bell pepper

½ teaspoon salt

¼ teaspoon black pepper

1 cup (4 ounces) shredded Cheddar cheese

1. Pour broth into **CROCK-POT®** slow cooker. Whisk in cornmeal. Add corn, chiles, bell pepper, salt and pepper. Cover; cook on LOW 4 to 5 hours or on HIGH 2 to 3 hours.

2. Stir in cheese. Continue cooking, uncovered, 15 to 30 minutes or until cheese melts.

Recipe courtesy of
Crock-Pot® Slow Cooker Kitchens

Not Your Gramma's Kugel

MAKES 6 SERVINGS

PREP TIME
10 MINUTES

COOK TIME
2 HOURS

Vegetable cooking spray

1 package (12 ounces) *uncooked* medium egg noodles (about 7 cups)

½ cup currants

1 can (10¾ ounces) **Campbell's**® Condensed Cheddar Cheese Soup

1 cup cottage cheese

¾ cup sugar

1 teaspoon grated orange zest

2 eggs

1. Spray the inside of a 3½-quart **CROCK-POT**® slow cooker with the cooking spray.

2. Cook the noodles according to the package directions until they're almost tender. Drain and place them in the **CROCK-POT**® slow cooker. Sprinkle with the currants.

3. Beat the soup, cottage cheese, sugar, orange zest and eggs in a medium bowl with a fork. Pour over the noodles and stir to coat.

4. Cover and cook on LOW for 2 to 2½ hours or until it's set. Serve warm.

tip

This versatile sweet noodle pudding can be served as a dessert, a brunch dish or a side dish alongside barbecued chicken or brisket.

Recipe courtesy of
Campbell's Kitchen

Barley with Currants and Pine Nuts

1 tablespoon unsalted butter

1 small onion, finely chopped

½ cup pearled barley

2 cups **Swanson**® Chicken Broth (Regular, **Natural Goodness**® *or* Certified Organic)

½ teaspoon salt, or to taste

¼ teaspoon black pepper

⅓ cup currants

¼ cup pine nuts

1. Melt butter in small skillet over medium-high heat. Add onion. Cook and stir until lightly browned, about 2 minutes. Transfer to **CROCK-POT**® slow cooker. Add barley, broth, salt and pepper. Stir in currants. Cover; cook on LOW 3 hours.

2. Stir in pine nuts and serve immediately.

Recipe courtesy of
Crock-Pot® Slow Cooker Kitchens

side dishes

216

Deluxe Potato Casserole

1 can (10¾ ounces) **Campbell's®** Condensed Cream of Chicken Soup (Regular *or* 98% Fat Free), undiluted

1 container (8 ounces) sour cream

¼ cup chopped onion

¼ cup *plus* 3 tablespoons melted butter, divided

1 teaspoon salt

2 pounds red potatoes, peeled and diced

2 cups (8 ounces) shredded Cheddar cheese

1½ to 2 cups stuffing mix

MAKES 8 TO 10 SERVINGS

COOK TIME
8 TO 10 HOURS (LOW)
OR
5 TO 6 HOURS (HIGH)

1. Combine soup, sour cream, onion, ¼ **cup** butter and salt in small bowl.

2. Combine potatoes and cheese in **CROCK-POT®** slow cooker. Pour soup mixture over potato mixture; mix well. Sprinkle stuffing mix over potato mixture; drizzle with remaining **3 tablespoons** butter. Cover; cook on LOW 8 to 10 hours or on HIGH 5 to 6 hours or until potatoes are tender.

Recipe courtesy of
Crock-Pot® Slow Cooker Kitchens

side dishes

217

Slow-Cooked Ratatouille with Penne

MAKES 4 SERVINGS

PREP TIME
25 MINUTES

COOK TIME
5 HOURS 30 MINUTES

1 can (10¾ ounces) **Campbell's**® Condensed Tomato Soup

1 tablespoon olive oil

⅛ teaspoon ground black pepper

1 small eggplant, peeled and cut into ½-inch cubes (about 5 cups)

1 medium zucchini, thinly sliced (about 1½ cups)

1 medium red pepper, diced (about 1 cup)

1 large onion, sliced (about 1 cup)

1 clove garlic, minced

Hot cooked penne pasta

Grated Parmesan cheese (optional)

1. Stir the soup, oil, black pepper, eggplant, zucchini, red pepper, onion and garlic in a 4-quart **CROCK-POT**® slow cooker.

2. Cover and cook on LOW for 5½ to 6 hours* or until the vegetables are tender.

3. Serve the vegetable mixture over the pasta. Sprinkle with the cheese, if desired.

Or on HIGH for 2½ to 3 hours.

Recipe courtesy of
Campbell's Kitchen

Wild Rice with Fruit & Nuts

side dishes

MAKES 6 TO 8 SERVINGS

PREP TIME
10 MINUTES

COOK TIME
7 HOURS (LOW)
OR
2½ TO 3 HOURS (HIGH)

2 cups wild rice (*or* wild rice blend), rinsed*

½ cup dried cranberries

½ cup chopped raisins

½ cup chopped dried apricots

½ cup almond slivers, toasted**

5 to 6 cups **Swanson**® Chicken Broth (Regular, **Natural Goodness**® *or* Certified Organic)

1 cup orange juice

2 tablespoons butter, melted

1 teaspoon ground cumin

2 green onions, thinly sliced

2 to 3 tablespoons chopped fresh parsley

Salt *and* black pepper, to taste

*Do not use parboiled rice or a blend containing parboiled rice.

**To toast almonds, spread in single layer in heavy-bottomed skillet. Cook over medium heat 1 to 2 minutes, stirring frequently, until nuts are lightly browned. Remove from skillet immediately. Cool before using.

1. Combine wild rice, cranberries, raisins, apricots and almonds in **CROCK-POT**® slow cooker.

2. Combine broth, orange juice, butter and cumin in medium bowl. Pour mixture over rice and stir to mix.

3. Cover; cook on LOW 7 hours or on HIGH 2½ to 3 hours. Stir once, adding more hot broth if necessary.

4. When rice is soft, add green onions and parsley. Adjust seasonings, if desired. Cook 10 minutes longer and serve.

Recipe courtesy of
Crock-Pot® *Slow Cooker*
Kitchens

CROCK·POT
· THE ORIGINAL SLOW COOKER ·

Campbell's

Greek Rice

MAKES 6 TO 8 SERVINGS

COOK TIME
4 HOURS (LOW)

2 tablespoons butter

1¾ cups *uncooked* converted long grain rice

2 cans (14 ounces *each*) **Swanson® Natural Goodness®** Chicken Broth

1 teaspoon Greek seasoning

1 teaspoon ground oregano

1 cup pitted kalamata olives, drained and chopped

¾ cup chopped roasted red peppers

Crumbled feta cheese (optional)

Chopped fresh Italian parsley (optional)

Melt butter in large nonstick skillet over medium-high heat. Add rice and sauté 4 minutes or until golden brown. Transfer to **CROCK-POT®** slow cooker. Stir in chicken broth, Greek seasoning and oregano. Cover and cook on LOW 4 hours or until liquid has all been absorbed and rice is tender. Stir in olives and roasted red peppers and cook 5 minutes more. Garnish with feta and Italian parsley, if desired.

Recipe courtesy of
Crock-Pot® Slow Cooker Kitchens

Scalloped Potatoes

Vegetable cooking spray

3 pounds Yukon Gold **or** Eastern potatoes, thinly sliced (about 9 cups)

1 large onion, thinly sliced (about 1 cup)

1 can (10¾ ounces) **Campbell's** Condensed Cream of Mushroom Soup (Regular **or** 98% Fat Free)

½ cup **Campbell's®** Condensed Chicken Broth

1 cup shredded Cheddar **or** crumbled blue cheese (about 4 ounces)

1. Spray the inside of a 6-quart **CROCK-POT®** slow cooker with the cooking spray. Layer **one third** of the potatoes and **half** of the onion in the **CROCK-POT®** slow cooker. Repeat the layers. Top with the remaining potatoes.

2. Stir the soup and broth in a small bowl. Pour over the potatoes. Cover and cook on HIGH for 4 to 5 hours or until the potatoes are tender.

3. Top the potatoes with the cheese. Cover and let stand for 5 minutes or until the cheese is melted.

side dishes

223

Recipe courtesy of
Campbell's Kitchen

Cheese Grits with Chiles and Bacon

6 strips bacon, divided

1 serrano **or** jalapeño pepper, cored, seeded and minced*

1 large shallot **or** small onion, finely chopped

1 cup grits**

4 cups **Swanson**® Chicken Broth (Regular, **Natural Goodness**® **or** Certified Organic)

¼ teaspoon black pepper

Salt, to taste

½ cup half-and-half

1 cup shredded Cheddar cheese

2 tablespoons finely chopped green onion, green part only

Hot peppers can sting and irritate the skin, so wear rubber gloves when handling peppers and do not touch your eyes.

**You may use coarse, instant, yellow or stone-ground grits.*

1. Fry bacon on both sides in medium skillet until crisp. Remove bacon and drain on paper towels. Cut **2** strips into bite-size pieces. Refrigerate and reserve remaining bacon. Place cut-up bacon in **CROCK-POT**® slow cooker.

2. Drain all but **1 tablespoon** bacon drippings in skillet. Add serrano pepper and shallot. Cook and stir over medium-high heat 1 minute or until shallot is transparent and lightly browned. Transfer to **CROCK-POT**® slow cooker. Stir in grits, broth, pepper and salt. Cover; cook on LOW 4 hours.

3. Stir in half-and-half and cheese. Sprinkle on green onions. Chop remaining bacon into bite-size pieces and stir into grits or sprinkle on top of **each** serving. Serve immediately.

side dishes

224

Recipe courtesy of
Crock-Pot® Slow Cooker Kitchens

Spinach Risotto

MAKES 4 SERVINGS

COOK TIME
2 TO 2½ HOURS (HIGH)

2 teaspoons butter

2 teaspoons olive oil

3 tablespoons finely chopped shallot

1¼ cups arborio rice

½ cup dry white wine

3 cups **Swanson**® Chicken Broth (Regular, **Natural Goodness**® *or* Certified Organic)

½ teaspoon salt

2 cups baby spinach

¼ cup grated Parmesan cheese

2 tablespoons pine nuts, toasted

1. Melt butter in medium skillet over medium heat; add oil. Add shallot and cook, stirring frequently, until softened but not browned.

2. Stir in rice and cook 2 to 3 minutes or until chalky and well coated. Stir in wine and cook until reduced by half. Transfer to **CROCK-POT**® slow cooker. Stir in broth and salt.

3. Cover and cook on HIGH 2 to 2½ hours or until rice is almost cooked but still contains a little liquid. Stir in spinach. Cover and cook 15 to 20 minutes or until spinach is cooked and rice is tender and creamy. Gently stir in Parmesan cheese and pine nuts just before serving.

Recipe courtesy of
Crock-Pot® Slow Cooker Kitchens

Cornbread Stuffing with Dried Fruit & Herbs

MAKES 24 SERVINGS

PREP TIME
15 MINUTES

COOK TIME
3 HOURS

Vegetable cooking spray

1 bag (16 ounces) **Pepperidge Farm**® Cornbread Stuffing

2 cups mixed dried fruit (apples, apricots, cranberries *and* pears)

2 stalks celery, diced (about 1 cup)

1 large red onion, diced (about 1 cup)

½ teaspoon poultry seasoning

¼ cup chopped fresh parsley

4 cups **Swanson**® Chicken Broth (Regular, **Natural Goodness**® *or* Certified Organic)

1. Spray the inside of a 6-quart **CROCK-POT**® slow cooker with the cooking spray. Stir the stuffing, fruit, celery, onion, poultry seasoning, parsley and broth lightly in the **CROCK-POT**® slow cooker.

2. Cover and cook on HIGH for 1 hour. Reduce the heat to LOW. Cover and cook for 2 hours. Fluff the stuffing mixture with a fork before serving.

Recipe courtesy of
Campbell's Kitchen

CROCK·POT
· THE ORIGINAL SLOW COOKER ·

Campbell's

Southwestern Bean Medley

1¾ cups **Swanson®** Vegetable Broth (Regular *or* Certified Organic)

1 tablespoon chili powder

1 teaspoon ground cumin

1 can (about 15 ounces) black beans, rinsed and drained

1 can (about 15 ounces) chickpeas (garbanzo beans), rinsed and drained

1 can (about 15 ounces) white kidney beans (cannellini), rinsed and drained

½ cup dried lentils

1 can (about 14.5 ounces) diced tomatoes and green chilies

Chopped fresh cilantro leaves

MAKES 8 SERVINGS

PREP TIME
10 MINUTES

COOK TIME
7 HOURS

1. Stir the broth, chili powder, cumin, black beans, chickpeas, white kidney beans and lentils in a 3½-quart **CROCK-POT®** slow cooker.

2. Cover and cook on LOW for 6 to 7 hours*.

3. Stir in the tomatoes and green chilies. Cover and cook for 1 hour or until the beans are tender. Sprinkle with the cilantro.

Or on HIGH for 3 to 4 hours.

side dishes

229

tip

For a complete meal, serve over hot cooked rice.

Recipe courtesy of
Campbell's Kitchen

Chorizo and Corn Bread Dressing

MAKES 4 TO 6 SERVINGS

PREP TIME
15 MINUTES

COOK TIME
7 HOURS (LOW) OR
3½ HOURS (HIGH)

½ pound chorizo sausage, removed from casings

1 can (10¾ ounces) **Campbell's®** Condensed Cream of Chicken Soup (Regular **or** 98% Fat Free), undiluted

1¾ cups **Swanson® Natural Goodness®** Chicken Broth

1 box (6 ounces) corn bread stuffing mix

1 cup chopped onions

1 cup diced, seeded red bell pepper

1 cup chopped celery

3 large eggs, lightly beaten

1 cup frozen corn

1. Lightly spray inside of **CROCK-POT®** slow cooker with nonstick cooking spray.

2. Cook chorizo in large skillet over medium-high heat until browned, stirring frequently to break up meat. Transfer to **CROCK-POT®** slow cooker with slotted spoon and return skillet to heat.

3. Whisk cream of chicken soup and chicken broth into drippings in skillet. Add remaining ingredients and stir until well blended. Stir into **CROCK-POT®** slow cooker. Cover and cook on LOW 7 hours or on HIGH 3½ hours.

Recipe courtesy of
Crock-Pot® Slow Cooker
Kitchens

desserts

Peach & Berry Cobbler

Vegetable cooking spray

1 package (16 ounces) frozen peach slices

1 package (16 ounces) frozen mixed berries (strawberries, blueberries **and** raspberries)

1 cup **V8 V-Fusion**® Peach Mango Juice

1 tablespoon cornstarch

1 teaspoon almond extract

1 package (18.25 ounces) yellow cake mix

1 stick butter (4 ounces), cut into pieces

Confectioners' sugar

1. Spray the inside of a 6-quart **CROCK-POT**® slow cooker with the cooking spray. Place the peaches and berries into the **CROCK-POT**® slow cooker.

2. Stir the juice, cornstarch and almond extract in a small bowl. Pour into the **CROCK-POT**® slow cooker.

3. Sprinkle the cake mix over the fruit mixture. Dot with the butter.

4. Layer **8** pieces of paper towel across the top of the **CROCK-POT**® slow cooker. Place the **CROCK-POT**® slow cooker cover on top*.

5. Cook on LOW for 4 to 5 hours** or until the fruit mixture boils and thickens and the topping is cooked through. Sprinkle with the confectioners' sugar.

*The paper towels will absorb any moisture that rises to the top of the **CROCK-POT**® slow cooker.

**Do not lift the cover on the cooker at all during the first 3 hours of the cook time.

Recipe courtesy of
Campbell's Kitchen

Gingerbread with Dried Cherries

MAKES 6 SERVINGS

PREP TIME
15 MINUTES

COOK TIME
2 TO 3 HOURS

Vegetable cooking spray

3 cups all-purpose flour

1 teaspoon baking powder

1 teaspoon baking soda

1 teaspoon ground cinnamon

1 teaspoon ground ginger

¼ teaspoon salt

¼ teaspoon allspice

1 cup (2 sticks) butter, softened

½ cup packed brown sugar

4 eggs

¾ cup molasses

1 cup **V8®** 100% Vegetable Juice

1 cup dried cherries

Whipped cream (optional)

1. Spray a 4-quart **CROCK·POT®** slow cooker with the cooking spray.

2. Stir the flour, baking powder, baking soda, cinnamon, ginger, salt and allspice in a medium bowl.

3. Place the butter and brown sugar into a large bowl. Beat with an electric mixer on medium speed until creamy. Beat in the eggs and molasses.

4. Reduce the speed to low. Alternately beat in the flour mixture and the vegetable juice. Stir in the cherries. Pour the batter into the **CROCK·POT®** slow cooker.

5. Cover and cook on HIGH for 2 to 3 hours or until a toothpick inserted in the center comes out with moist crumbs. Spoon the gingerbread into bowls. Top with the whipped cream, if desired.

Recipe courtesy of
Campbell's Kitchen

Apple Cherry Pastries with Vanilla Cream

MAKES 12 SERVINGS

PREP TIME
30 MINUTES

COOK TIME
4 HOURS

8 apples (about 3 pounds), peeled and cut into ¼-inch slices

½ cup dried cherries

1 cup sugar

½ teaspoon grated lemon zest

2 packages (10 ounces *each*) **Pepperidge Farm**® Puff Pastry Shells

1 package (3.4 ounces) vanilla instant pudding and pie filling mix

3 cups milk

1. Stir the apples, cherries, sugar and lemon zest in a 4-quart **CROCK-POT**® slow cooker.

2. Cover and cook on LOW for 4 to 5 hours or until the apples are tender.

3. Bake, cool and remove the "tops" of the pastry shells according to the package directions.

4. Beat the pudding mix and milk in a medium bowl with a whisk for about 2 minutes or until the mixture is thickened.

5. Divide the apple mixture among the pastry shells. Spoon the pudding mixture over the apple mixture.

tip

*You can try substituting other flavors of pudding for the vanilla, such as lemon **or** even cheesecake!*

Recipe courtesy of
Campbell's Kitchen

Chocolate Cappuccino Bread Pudding

Vegetable cooking spray

1 loaf (24 ounces) **Pepperidge Farm Farmhouse**™ Hearty White Bread, cut into cubes (about 15 cups)

4 cups milk

¼ cup heavy cream

6 large eggs

1 tablespoon vanilla extract

1 cup granulated sugar

1 cup packed light brown sugar

¼ cup unsweetened cocoa powder

1 tablespoon instant espresso powder

1 cup semi-sweet chocolate pieces

1. Spray the inside of a 6-quart **CROCK-POT**® slow cooker with the cooking spray. Place the bread cubes into the **CROCK-POT**® slow cooker.

2. Beat the milk, cream, eggs and vanilla with a fork in a large bowl.

3. Stir the granulated sugar, brown sugar, cocoa powder and espresso powder in a medium bowl. Stir into the milk mixture.

4. Pour the milk mixture over the bread cubes. Stir and press the bread cubes into the milk mixture to coat. Sprinkle with the chocolate pieces.

5. Cover and cook on HIGH for 2 to 3 hours or until set.

MAKES 8 SERVINGS
PREP TIME
20 MINUTES
COOK TIME
2 HOURS

tip

*Serve warm with whipped cream **or** vanilla ice cream, **and** topped with toasted chopped almonds **or** pecans.*

Recipe courtesy of **Campbell's Kitchen**

The Claus's Christmas Pudding

MAKES 12 SERVINGS

PREP TIME
30 TO 35 MINUTES

COOK TIME
5½ HOURS (LOW)

Pudding

⅔ cup sweetened dried cranberries

⅔ cup golden raisins

½ cup whole candied red cherries, halved

¾ cup *plus* 2 tablespoons cream sherry, divided

18 slices cranberry **or** other fruited bread

3 large egg yolks, beaten

1½ cups light cream

⅓ cup granulated sugar

¼ teaspoon kosher salt

1½ teaspoons cherry extract

1 cup white chocolate chips

1 cup hot water

Sauce

2 large egg yolks, beaten

¼ cup powdered sugar, sifted

¼ teaspoon vanilla

½ cup whipping cream

Prepare Pudding

1. Preheat oven to 250°F. Generously butter 6½-cup ceramic or glass bowl. Place cranberries and raisins in small bowl; set aside. Place cherries in another bowl. Heat **¾ cup** sherry until warm, and pour over cherries; set aside.

2. Place bread slices on baking sheet and bake 5 minutes. Turn over and bake 5 minutes or until bread is dry. Cool, then cut into ½-inch cubes.

3. Combine egg yolks, light cream, granulated sugar and salt in heavy saucepan. Cook and stir over medium heat until mixture coats metal spoon. Remove from heat. Set saucepan in sink of ice water to cool quickly; stir 1 to 2 minutes. Stir in cherry extract. Transfer cooled mixture to large bowl. Fold bread cubes into custard until coated.

4. Drain cherries, reserving sherry. Arrange **one fourth** of cherries, plus ⅓ **cup** raisin mixture and ¼ **cup** white chocolate chips in prepared ceramic bowl. Add **one fourth** of bread cube mixture. Sprinkle with reserved sherry. Repeat layers 3 times, arranging fruit near edges of bowl. Pour remaining reserved sherry over all.

5. Cover bowl tightly with foil. Place in **CROCK-POT®** slow cooker. Pour hot water around bowl. Cover; cook on LOW 5½ hours. Remove bowl and let stand on wire rack 10 to 15 minutes before unmolding.

Prepare Sauce

6. Combine **2** egg yolks, powdered sugar, **2 tablespoons** sherry and vanilla. Beat whipping cream in small bowl until small peaks form. Fold whipped cream into egg yolk mixture. Cover; chill until serving time. Serve with warm pudding.

Recipe courtesy of
Crock-Pot® Slow Cooker Kitchens

English Bread Pudding

MAKES 6 TO 8 SERVINGS

COOK TIME
3½ TO 4 HOURS (LOW)

16 slices day-old, **Pepperidge Farm**® White Bread (1 small loaf)

1¾ cups milk

1 package (8 ounces) mixed dried fruit, cut into small pieces

½ cup chopped nuts

1 medium apple, chopped

⅓ cup packed brown sugar

¼ cup (½ stick) butter, melted

1 egg, lightly beaten

1 teaspoon ground cinnamon

¼ teaspoon ground nutmeg

¼ teaspoon ground cloves

1. Tear bread, with crusts, into 1- to 2-inch pieces; place in **CROCK-POT**® slow cooker. Pour milk over bread; let soak 30 minutes. Stir in dried fruit, nuts and apple.

2. Combine remaining ingredients in small bowl; pour over bread mixture. Stir well to blend. Cover; cook on LOW 3½ to 4 hours or until skewer inserted into center of pudding comes out clean.

tip

Chopping dried fruits can be difficult. To make the job easier, cut fruit with kitchen scissors. Spray scissors (or your chef's knife) with nonstick cooking spray before chopping, to prevent sticking.

Recipe courtesy of
Crock-Pot® Slow Cooker Kitchens

Blueberry Compote with Lemon Dumplings

2 pounds frozen blueberries

¾ cup sugar

1 cup **V8 V-Fusion**® Pomegranate Blueberry Juice

2 cups buttermilk baking mix

⅔ cup milk

1 tablespoon grated lemon zest

Vanilla ice cream (optional)

1. Stir the blueberries, **½ cup** sugar and juice in a 4-quart **CROCK-POT**® slow cooker.

2. Cover and cook on LOW for 3 to 4 hours or until the mixture boils and thickens.

3. Stir the baking mix, remaining sugar, milk and lemon zest in a small bowl. Drop the batter by rounded tablespoonfuls over the blueberry mixture.

4. Cover and cook on HIGH for 20 minutes or until the dumplings are cooked in the center. Serve with the vanilla ice cream, if desired.

MAKES 8 SERVINGS

PREP TIME
10 MINUTES

COOK TIME
3 HOURS 20 MINUTES

tip

If you don't have a fresh lemon on hand for the lemon zest, try orange or lime zest instead.

Recipe courtesy of
Campbell's Kitchen

THE ORIGINAL SLOW COOKER

Five-Spice Apple Crisp

MAKES 4 SERVINGS

COOK TIME
3½ HOURS (LOW)

3 tablespoons unsalted butter, melted

6 Golden Delicious apples, peeled, cored and cut into ½-inch-thick slices

2 teaspoons fresh lemon juice

¼ cup packed light brown sugar

¾ teaspoon Chinese five-spice powder *or* ½ teaspoon ground cinnamon *and* ¼ teaspoon ground allspice

1 cup coarsely crushed Chinese-style almond cookies *or* almond biscotti

Sweetened whipped cream (optional)

1. Brush 4½-quart **CROCK-POT®** slow cooker with melted butter. Add apples and lemon juice and toss to combine. Sprinkle with brown sugar and five-spice powder and toss again.

2. Cover; cook for 3½ hours on LOW or until apples are tender. Sprinkle cookies over apples. Spoon into bowls and serve warm, garnished with whipped cream, if desired.

Recipe courtesy of
Crock-Pot® Slow Cooker
Kitchens

Triple Chocolate Pudding Cake with Raspberry Sauce

Vegetable cooking spray

1 package (about 18 ounces) chocolate cake mix

1 package (about 3.9 ounces) chocolate instant pudding and pie filling mix

2 cups sour cream

4 eggs

1 cup **V8**® 100% Vegetable Juice

¾ cup vegetable oil

1 cup semi-sweet chocolate pieces

Raspberry dessert topping

Whipped cream

MAKES 12 SERVINGS

PREP TIME
10 MINUTES

COOK TIME
6 HOURS

desserts

243

1. Spray the inside of a 4-quart **CROCK-POT**® slow cooker with the cooking spray.

2. Beat the cake mix, pudding mix, sour cream, eggs, vegetable juice and oil in a large bowl with an electric mixer on medium speed for 2 minutes. Stir in the chocolate pieces. Pour the batter into the **CROCK-POT**® slow cooker.

3. Cover and cook on LOW for 6 to 7 hours or until a knife inserted in the center comes out with moist crumbs. Serve with the raspberry topping and whipped cream.

tip

Use your favorite chocolate cake mix and pudding mix flavor in this recipe: chocolate, devil's food, dark chocolate or chocolate fudge.

Recipe courtesy of
Campbell's Kitchen

Cinnamon Breakfast Bread Pudding

MAKES 6 SERVINGS

PREP TIME
15 MINUTES

COOK TIME
4 HOURS

Vegetable cooking spray

1 loaf (16 ounces) **Pepperidge Farm**® Raisin Cinnamon Swirl Bread, cut into cubes

4 eggs

3½ cups milk

1 cup *plus* 1 tablespoon packed brown sugar

1 tablespoon vanilla extract

¾ teaspoon ground cinnamon

Maple-flavored syrup

1. Spray the inside of a 4- to 6-quart **CROCK-POT**® slow cooker with the cooking spray. Place the bread cubes into the **CROCK-POT**® slow cooker.

2. Beat the eggs, milk, **1 cup** of the brown sugar, vanilla and ½ **teaspoon** of the cinnamon with a fork in a large bowl. Pour into the **CROCK-POT**® slow cooker. Stir and press bread cubes into the milk mixture to coat. Sprinkle with the remaining brown sugar and cinnamon.

3. Cover and cook on LOW for 4 to 5 hours* or until set. Serve warm with maple syrup.

Or on HIGH for 2 to 3 hours.

Recipe courtesy of
Campbell's Kitchen

Brown Sugar Spice Cake

Vegetable cooking spray

1 can (10¾ ounces) **Campbell's**® Condensed Tomato Soup (Regular **or** Healthy Request®)

½ cup water

2 eggs

1 box (about 18 ounces) spice cake mix

1¼ cups hot water

¾ cup packed brown sugar

1 teaspoon ground cinnamon

Vanilla ice cream

1. Spray the inside of a 4-quart **CROCK-POT**® slow cooker with the cooking spray.

2. Combine the soup, water, eggs and cake mix in a medium bowl and mix according to the package directions. Pour the batter into the **CROCK-POT**® slow cooker.

3. Stir the water, brown sugar and cinnamon in a small bowl. Pour over the batter.

4. Cover and cook on HIGH for 2 hours or until a knife inserted in the center comes out clean.

5. Spoon the cake into bowls, spooning the sauce from the bottom of the **CROCK-POT**® slow cooker. Serve warm with the ice cream.

MAKES 8 SERVINGS
PREP TIME
10 MINUTES
COOK TIME
2 HOURS

tip

This warm, gooey dessert would be great sprinkled with crunchy candied walnuts.

Recipe courtesy of **Campbell's Kitchen**

Raisin Cinnamon Bread Pudding

MAKES 6 SERVINGS

PREP TIME
10 MINUTES

COOK TIME
2 HOURS 30 MINUTES

Vegetable cooking spray

10 slices **Pepperidge Farm**® Raisin Cinnamon Swirl Bread, cut into cubes (about 5 cups)

1 can (14 ounces) sweetened condensed milk

1 cup water

1 teaspoon vanilla extract

4 eggs, beaten

Ice cream (optional)

1. Spray the inside of a 4½- to 5-quart **CROCK-POT**® slow cooker with the cooking spray.

2. Place the bread cubes into the **CROCK-POT**® slow cooker.

3. Beat the milk, water, vanilla and eggs with a fork in a medium bowl. Pour over the bread mixture. Stir and press the bread cubes into the milk mixture to coat.

4. Cover and cook on LOW for 2½ to 3 hours or until set. Serve warm with the ice cream, if desired.

Recipe courtesy of
Campbell's Kitchen

Harvest Fruit Compote

1 lemon

2 packages (12 ounces **each**) prunes (about 4 cups)

1 package (7 ounces) mixed dried fruit (about 1½ cups)

1 package (about 6 ounces) dried apricots (about 1½ cups)

½ cup dried cranberries

⅓ cup raisins

4 cups **V8 V-Fusion**® Pomegranate Blueberry Juice

1 cup white Zinfandel wine

1 teaspoon vanilla extract

1. Grate **1 teaspoon** zest from the lemon.

2. Stir the prunes, mixed fruit, apricots, cranberries, raisins, juice, wine, lemon zest and vanilla in a 6-quart **CROCK-POT**® slow cooker.

3. Cover and cook on HIGH for 4 to 5 hours*.

*Or on LOW for 7 to 8 hours.

MAKES 10 SERVINGS
PREP TIME
10 MINUTES
COOK TIME
4 HOURS

tip

The compote can be served warm or cold. Try it warm spooned over vanilla ice cream or pound cake. Try it warm or cold as an accompaniment to roast pork loin.

Recipe courtesy of
Campbell's Kitchen

Pumpkin-Cranberry Custard

MAKES 4 TO 6 SERVINGS

COOK TIME
4 TO 4½ HOURS (HIGH)

1 can (30 ounces) pumpkin pie filling

1 can (12 ounces) evaporated milk

1 cup dried cranberries

4 eggs, beaten

1 cup crushed or whole gingersnap cookies, crushed **or** whole (optional)

Whipped cream (optional)

Combine pumpkin, evaporated milk, cranberries and eggs in **CROCK-POT®** slow cooker; mix thoroughly. Cover; cook on HIGH 4 to 4½ hours. Serve with crushed or whole gingersnaps and whipped cream, if desired.

Recipe courtesy of
Crock-Pot® Slow Cooker Kitchens

Tropical Pudding Cake

2 cups all-purpose flour

⅔ cup sugar

2 teaspoons baking powder

1 teaspoon ground cinnamon

8 tablespoons butter, melted

1 cup milk

1 can (21 ounces) canned sliced apples

1 can (20 ounces) crushed pineapple, drained

¾ cup toasted walnuts

2 cups packed brown sugar

2 cups **V8 Splash**® Tropical Blend Juice Drink

2 cups water

Vanilla ice cream (optional)

MAKES 8 SERVINGS

PREP TIME
15 MINUTES

COOK TIME
2 HOURS

STAND TIME
30 MINUTES

Recipe courtesy of
Campbell's Kitchen

1. Stir the flour, sugar, baking powder and cinnamon in a large bowl. Stir **half** of the butter and the milk into the flour mixture. Stir the apples, pineapple and walnuts into the batter. Pour into a 4-quart **CROCK-POT**® slow cooker.

2. Heat the brown sugar, juice drink, water and remaining butter in a 3-quart saucepan over medium-high heat to a boil. Cook for 2 minutes, stirring often. Pour over the batter in the **CROCK-POT**® slow cooker.

3. Cover and cook on HIGH for 2 to 3 hours or until a toothpick inserted in the center comes out with moist crumbs.

4. Turn off the **CROCK-POT**® slow cooker. Uncover and let stand for 30 minutes. Serve with vanilla ice cream, if desired.

Homestyle Apple Brown Betty

MAKES 8 SERVINGS

PREP TIME
15 MINUTES

COOK TIME
3 TO 4 HOURS (LOW)
OR
2 HOURS (HIGH)

6 cups of your favorite cooking apples, peeled, cored and cut into eighths

1 cup bread crumbs

1 teaspoon ground cinnamon

1 teaspoon ground nutmeg

⅛ teaspoon salt

¾ cup packed brown sugar

½ cup (1 stick) butter *or* margarine, melted

¼ cup finely chopped walnuts

1. Lightly grease **CROCK-POT**® slow cooker. Place apples on bottom.

2. Combine bread crumbs, cinnamon, nutmeg, salt, brown sugar, butter and walnuts, and spread over apples.

3. Cover; cook on LOW 3 to 4 hours or on HIGH 2 hours.

tip

*Expecting a crowd? Just double the amounts of all the ingredients and prepare in a 5-, 6- or 7-quart **CROCK-POT**® slow cooker.*

Recipe courtesy of
Crock-Pot® Slow Cooker Kitchens

index

index

Pork

Poultry

Metric Conversion Chart

VOLUME MEASUREMENTS (dry)

⅛ teaspoon = 0.5 mL
¼ teaspoon = 1 mL
½ teaspoon = 2 mL
¾ teaspoon = 4 mL
1 teaspoon = 5 mL
1 tablespoon = 15 mL
2 tablespoons = 30 mL
¼ cup = 60 mL
⅓ cup = 75 mL
½ cup = 125 mL
⅔ cup = 150 mL
¾ cup = 175 mL
1 cup = 250 mL
2 cups = 1 pint = 500 mL
3 cups = 750 mL
4 cups = 1 quart = 1 L

VOLUME MEASUREMENTS (fluid)

1 fluid ounce (2 tablespoons) = 30 mL
4 fluid ounces (½ cup) = 125 mL
8 fluid ounces (1 cup) = 250 mL
12 fluid ounces (1½ cups) = 375 mL
16 fluid ounces (2 cups) = 500 mL

WEIGHTS (mass)

½ ounce = 15 g
1 ounce = 30 g
3 ounces = 90 g
4 ounces = 120 g
8 ounces = 225 g
10 ounces = 285 g
12 ounces = 360 g
16 ounces = 1 pound = 450 g

DIMENSIONS

1/16 inch = 2 mm
⅛ inch = 3 mm
¼ inch = 6 mm
½ inch = 1.5 cm
¾ inch = 2 cm
1 inch = 2.5 cm

OVEN TEMPERATURES

250°F = 120°C
275°F = 140°C
300°F = 150°C
325°F = 160°C
350°F = 180°C
375°F = 190°C
400°F = 200°C
425°F = 220°C
450°F = 230°C

BAKING PAN AND DISH EQUIVALENTS

Utensil	Size in Inches	Size in Centimeters	Volume	Metric Volume
Baking or Cake Pan (square or rectangular)	8×8×2	20×20×5	8 cups	2 L
	9×9×2	23×23×5	10 cups	2.5 L
	13×9×2	33×23×5	12 cups	3 L
Loaf Pan	8½×4½×2½	21×11×6	6 cups	1.5 L
	9×9×3	23×13×7	8 cups	2 L
Round Layer Cake Pan	8×1½	20×4	4 cups	1 L
	9×1½	23×4	5 cups	1.25 L
Pie Plate	8×1½	20×4	4 cups	1 L
	9×1½	23×4	5 cups	1.25 L
Baking Dish or Casserole			1 quart/4 cups	1 L
			1½ quart/6 cups	1.5 L
			2 quart/8 cups	2 L
			3 quart/12 cups	3 L

CROCK·POT.
· THE ORIGINAL SLOW COOKER ·

Campbell's